PETER G. FILENE teaches a course in American women's history and has written numerous articles on woman's history and sex roles. He is also the author of a previous book, *HIM/HER/SELF: Sex Roles in Modern America*.

Peter G. Filene teaches a course in American women's history and has written numerous articles on women's history and sex roles. He is also the author of a previous book, *Him/Her/Self: Sex Roles in Modern America.*

MEN IN THE MIDDLE

COPING WITH THE PROBLEMS OF WORK & FAMILY IN THE LIVES OF MIDDLE-AGED MEN

PETER FILENE

A SPECTRUM BOOK

PRENTICE-HALL, INC., Englewood Cliffs, New Jersey 07632

Library of Congress Cataloging in Publication Data

Main entry under title:
Men in the middle.

(A Spectrum Book)
Includes bibliographical references.
1. Middle aged men—United States—Biography.
2. Middle classes—United States—Addresses, essays,
lectures.   3. Masculinity (Psychology)—Addresses, essays,
lectures.   I. Filene, Peter G.
HQ1059.5.U5M45   305.2'4   81–2865
ISBN 0–13–574509–8   AACR2
ISBN 0–13–574491–1 (pbk.)

This Spectrum Book can be made available
to businesses and organizations at a
special discount when ordered in large
quantities. For more information, contact
Prentice-Hall, Inc., General Book Marketing,
Special Sales Division, Englewood Cliffs,
New Jersey 07632

10   9   8   7   6   5   4   3   2   1

Printed in the United States of America

Editorial/production supervision by Pat Lewis
Manufacturing buyer: Cathie Lenard

Prentice-Hall International, Inc., *London*
Prentice-Hall of Australia Pty., *Limited, Sydney*
Prentice-Hall of Canada, Ltd., *Toronto*
Prentice-Hall of India Private, Limited, *New Delhi*
Prentice-Hall of Japan, Inc., *Tokyo*
Prentice-Hall of Southeast Asia Pte., Ltd., *Singapore*
Whitehall Books Limited, *Wellington, New Zealand*

Contents

Acknowledgments

This has been in many ways a collaborative book. Most obviously and most importantly, it has emerged from the commitments of its contributors. But I want to mention what is not obvious: namely, the exceptional loyalty of my fellow authors. These seven men wrote and rewrote their essays before knowing that all their effort would be rewarded by publication. In writing, moreover, they took the risk of honesty. And finally, during the times when I lost clarity or hope about this venture, they gave me invaluable guidance and encouragement.

Many people generously consented to read some or all of the manuscript. Their sensitive, acute comments helped immeasurably to improve what we wrote. In particular I want to thank Lynne Barrett, Pamela Daniels, Joe Dubbert, John Kasson, Kathy Meads, Joseph Pleck, Daryl Walker, and Peter Walker. I am grateful to Laurie Christesen and Rosalie Radcliffe for having typed the manuscript with care and efficiency. I owe a special debt to Barbara Plumb for having encouraged me to begin this book, and to Joseph Pleck for having been instrumental in finding a publisher for it. Patricia Rieker deserves particularly emphatic thanks because her insights, so sharp and so compassionate, gave me the perspective I needed to write the introduction. Finally, I think William Chafe, who provided advice as well as friendship at a time when I needed them most.

I would also like to acknowledge, with appreciation, permission to use the following:

The poem "To My Son" is used by permission of Janet C. Boyte.

The poem "Wallet" from Robert Hahn, *Routine Risks*—Omaha Nebr.: Abbatoir Editrions, 1976—is used by permission of the author.

Two poems from Robert Hahn, *Crimes,* published by Lynx House Press in 1976, are used by permission of the author.

The excerpt from William Carlos Williams, *Imaginations* is reprinted by permission of New Directions and Laurence Pollinger, Ltd. Copyright © 1923 by William Carlos Williams, copyright © 1970 by Florence H. Williams.

The photograph of Steve Turner is used by permission of The Picture Group, Inc., Don Abood. © 1980 LIONEL DELEVINGNE/ PICTURE GROUP.

The line from "Home Again" by Carole King is used by permission. Copyright © 1971 by COLGEMS-EMI MUSIC INC. All rights reserved.

The photograph of Tom Kreilkamp is used by permission of John B. Newell.

Photographs of Harry Boyte, Peter Filene, Arn Strasser, Robert Hahn, and Lawrence Rubin were taken by Peter Filene.

Peter Filene
Pittsboro, North Carolina

1
Introducing Ourselves

by Peter Filene

The men you will meet in this book are not national celebrities. None of us has skied down Everest, made a million dollars, or won the Nobel Prize. Few of us are even heroes of lesser proportions. Although in the following pages you will encounter courage, triumph, and insight, you will also find many instances of confusion, regret, failure, or simply numb floating in the current of events.

We are not extraordinary, but neither are our subjects: work and family. What meaning or satisfaction have men sought from their occupations and their home lives? How much have they found? And how much coherence have they made between the world of work and the world of home? These are the questions with which the essayists have contended. It is this wrestle with questions, rather than the victory of answers, that forms the central purpose of our book. In fact, if there is any heroism here, it occurs in these men's daring to face themselves and ask honestly "why" or "why not."

We are men in the middle. We belong to the middle class, although some of us began lower than others, and some of us have risen higher. We also belong to middle age, born between 1934 and 1945. But the important coincidence among us is not biological so much as it is emotional, for we are also in the middle of large questions, those profoundly unsettling "life questions" that come to a man just when he believes he has found answers about how to be a "grown-up." Conceivably this upheaval can occur somewhat earlier or later; for us it occurred a few years before or after the age of forty.

Eight men near the midpoint of their lives, each looking back on what he has achieved or forsaken in the worlds of work and home, each taking stock in preparation for his next half of life—that is who we are and why we have convened in this book. Because our lives, like most lives, have moved along unexalted planes, we believe that our essays will speak recognizably to other men (and women, too).

As you will see, we agree on the questions but not on the answers. This is not a book of doctrine; it is a book of choice. Starting with the same set of questions, the essays move toward diverse answers, as diverse as the authors and our readers. It is a book of multiple choice because, we believe, people cast their lives in many different forms according to choices taken, spurned, or misunderstood.

HOW IT BEGAN

This book began in 1977 as an echo to a volume of essays by twenty-three educated middle-class women—most of them wives and mothers—focusing on the problem of how to choose work and place it in the forefront of their lives.[1] *Working It Out* is basically a collection of success stories. Each women relates how she overcame social discrimination, personal anxieties, and the brambles of daily circumstances until finally acquiring meaningful work. *Work-*

ing It Out is also a collective success story. It could not have been written ten years earlier, because the woman's movement had not yet taken shape. The insights and strengths of these twenty-three women were distilled from the millions of women who talked in consciousness-raising groups, who debated in feminist organizations, who lobbied in legislatures, who wrote pamphlets and poems, manifestoes and novels, all demanding that women have the same employment opportunities as men.

That is the egalitarian argument from the female viewpoint. But hold it up to a mirror and suddenly you see the principle of equal opportunity in a new, perplexing form. For men, work is already a built-in part of their conventional role. It is not a right so much as a fact of life. The economic "news" attends to unemployment rates for men, employment rates for women. In contrast to the women's liberation movement, a men's liberation movement would not demand the right to work. But if not that, then what?

When mirror logic reverses the familiar principle of sexual equality, one faces questions that are quite unfamiliar. How have men fitted (or not fitted) marriage and parenthood into their lives along with work? And to what extent have they acquired (or not acquired) fulfillment from these spheres of their daily life? Feminists have intensified American concern with women's search for equal opportunity and full personal development. The concern surely is as important for the other half of the population. As important, but more neglected. Hence this book.

WHO

Toward the end of 1977 I sent letters to twenty friends, friends of friends, and men whom I knew only through their publications, asking each to write an autobiographical essay about the role of work and family in his life. To provide them some structure for a potentially shapeless assignment, I suggested three themes: *achievement* ("What have you done? What have you thought and felt about what you have done?"); *relationships* ("Which people have made a difference in your life?"); and *life cycle* ("Do these activities and relationships form a pattern of phases and turning points?"). I urged the contributors to write personally and specifically, leaving general analysis to my introduction.

All the men whom I solicited were between the ages of thirty-six and forty-five, all college-educated, and in business or a profession. Although I strove for occupational, geographical, and marital diversity, my primary criterion was to find men who have given thought—hard thought and also soft feelings—to the meanings of their lives. The venture's success depended not on social/scientific rigor but on the luminosity of self-perceptions.

I invited by hunch. Half of the twenty men have been my friends for many years. I knew they had undergone significant changes in marriage and career, and that along the way they had achieved insights that would be instructive to other men. I did not know, however, whether they could translate those insights effectively to paper. As for the other contributors, whom I knew less clearly or only secondhand, I would just have to wait for their essays before deciding how well they would serve.

I was prepared, then, for results of varying quality. But I was unprepared—in fact, confused and dismayed—by the kinds of responses that came back. Three men said "maybe," doubting whether they would have sufficient time or sufficient insight, and in the end they wrote nothing. Two made no response at all, even after I sent a follow-up letter. Three said "no" in different ways. "My life is so ordinary, strictly dullsville, that I don't see how it could interest anyone else," one man replied, "unless I reveal intimacies, which I won't." Another said: "I would feel comfortable only if I could use a pseudonym and disguise my identity." And after six months, a third man: "I'm plainly not going to come through, and feel lousy about it. I have felt more and more negative toward myself over the course of the spring, and finally doubt that I can produce anything for you unless you have a section on 'coming apart.' Probably with more guts I could have toughed this one out and put together something that would have been okay. But I guess that at bottom I don't now want to know where I am."

Twelve said "yes," in several cases adding: "Whether or not this is ever published, I'm glad for the opportunity to come to terms with these questions. Thanks." During the subsequent year, however, five of these "yeses" turned into apologetic promises or total silences, but never essays.

This mélange of response probably is typical of any team publishing effort. Good men—even good men with good intentions—don't always produce good results. Time is short; business or children or wives or relaxation pull more strongly than the invitation to write for a book that may or may not see the light of day. Moreover, writing about oneself—particularly if it is to be honest writing—poses difficulty. When I began my own autobiographical essay, I appreciated just how difficult. What to say, what not to say, how to say it, is this interesting, is this honest, is this really me? As one contributor scribbled in a note accompanying his finished essay: "Here it is at last. Glad to be done with it. Toughest thing I ever wrote." And he had written and published much else.

Competing obligations and the nature of the task account for much of the "no show" rate. Nevertheless, I also can't help seeing implications that touch the theme of the book itself. For one thing, "being too busy" may be not only a rival for a man's attention to a personal dilemma; it may be part and parcel of the dilemma. In other words, not simply excuse, but symptom. According to numerous surveys, up-and-coming men—especially those who control their own schedules and those in the professions—work far longer than the average American's forty hours per week. One fourth of these men log fifty-five hours or more, one sixth log sixty or more, subordinating almost everything else to work, including the opportunity to think about whether work is satisfaction or obsession.[2] Beyond that consequence upon themselves, their devotion to work loads a consequence upon their marriages. According to one study of middle-class men across a thirty-year span, the more successful they became in their occupations, the more dissatisfaction developed between them and their wives.[3] Men's work can serve not simply as a postponement of facing personal dilemmas; it can produce those dilemmas.

I find a second "male meaning" in the no-response of my contributors. Autobiography with only half of one's life enacted becomes as much forecast as retrospect. These men were being asked to tell their own fortunes, future as well as past. That can be tricky, and risky. From such a reckoning one can find clarification and confidence. On the other hand, one can also tear up page after page of incoherent prose, enlarging the confusion that one set out to dispel. Midlife autobiography is like changing clothes while driving a car—a process hovering between acrobatics and wreck. Some contributors emerged victorious and, as Paul Fiddleman puts it, "like any survivor and veteran, I have bragging rights." Others survived to complete their essays but confess that they have reached no destination. Fiddleman may be "over the hump," but Robert Hahn asks: "Excuse me, but is this the way to the plateau?" Still other contributors never arrived even this far, concluding amid the same wordlessness where they began. As you read the eight essays in this book, think of the twelve never written—those two or three hundred blank pages that tell of men who did not see what they must work out or who saw all too much.

WHAT
Doing

The occupational patterns of the eight authors form no pattern. Robert Hahn, Harry Boyte, Tom Kreilkamp and I chose our lines of work before the age of twenty-one, but Hahn and Boyte have since amended or abandoned theirs, while Kreilkamp and I have not. Steve Turner and Paul Fiddleman entered careers in their mid- or late twenties, after Army service and other explorations. Arn Strasser and Lanny Rubin waited until their thirties before finding a vocation.

Each of us heard a different starting gun, and having run in bursts of zeal and lethargy, we are dispersed at all points of the occupational course. An anarchists' race, it would seem. But there is something else to be said, which is far from anarchist. We share the running track beneath us; it unites our apparent disarray. Whether we have "settled" the career question, or have reopened it, or are wrestling frantically with it, none of us has ignored it. Occupation has preoccupied our imaginations and our energies. It dominates each of these self-portraits. As Steve Turner writes: "John Calvin's hooks were sunk deep within us."

The discontinuity of career lines may be untypical of most middle-class men. As yet, sociologists and economists provide no confident generalization.[4] Certainly, though, the emphasis on work has been very much a typically male characteristic. Whereas most teenage girls of the 1950s dreamed of a future centered around a husband, most teenage boys sketched their futures in terms of employment. A man is what he does, and his doing takes place out in the world of work.[5]

Occupational "doing" forms only half of the story, of course. This book's theme centers on how men have fit work *and family* into their lives—a bifocal vision. As it turned out, however, several authors submitted monocular essays, almost losing sight of lovers, wives, children, and private activities. I called this one-sidedness to their attention and suggested that they make their stories more complete. The supplementary paragraphs or pages came back a few weeks later, accompanied by surprise ("you're right, I wonder why I hadn't noticed the omission") and reflection ("I added the material on family, but I can't see how to fit it closely with the rest"). In short, their essays exemplified the very question that the authors were trying to come to terms with.

Work consumes much more than half of these men's attention, and sometimes it coexists quite uneasily with family. This is a salient pattern. There is also a counterpattern, covert but important. In many of these life stories, work involves not simply paid employment, but doings of a very different sort. Riffle through the following pages, for example, and notice how often the continent of margin-to-margin prose opens up for an island of poetry. Amid their serious careers, many contributors have kept space free for serious play of the spirit. Arn Strasser still shelters the dream of an artist's studio, even as he has just established his medical office. When Lawrence Rubin plays the saxophone, he cannot hear the business messages clattering in on his Telex. These activities have no ulterior motive of promotion or income; they are their own reward. Or to use sociological jargon, they are not instrumental, but expressive—on the "feminine" rather than "masculine" side of stereotype.

I find that same quality in the substance of what these authors are expressing. Their avocations tend away from the "masculine" and toward the "feminine" half of the spectrum, away from hunting and ice hockey and auto mechanics toward art and cooking. Moreover, the expressions themselves are gentle rather than aggressive. It need not have been that way. This expressive current, whether eddying easily among their other activities or running volcanically deep underground, could have seethed with competition, violence, and other forms of machismo. If there is repression in these men's lives, it would seem to dam wishes to be not more of a man, but more than just a "manly" man.

Feeling

Emotions spill upon these pages. Arn Strasser weeps with the wound of Marian's betrayal; I weep with longing for the children I left; Harry Boyte weeps with relief at having confessed fears of power. And there are other moods: Robert Hahn sledding joyfully down a hill with his daughter; Tom Kreilkamp arguing with his wife about money; Steve Turner walking out of the cannery into the cool dawn, proud of his dusty, aching muscles.

These and other examples do not add up, however. On balance, these stories do not surge with feelings. I hate to say that. For many months I resisted saying it, loudly denied it. But finally I had to acknowledge what I was hearing so consistently from the people to whom I showed the manuscript. Whether friends or colleagues or editors, male or female, they all remarked on the guarded, analytic, cool style. Yes, these men wrote in the first person and, yes, they seemed to be honest. But my readers nevertheless said the words formed an opaque surface, a public mask through which they could not see to the private, vulnerable personality. "Where is the pain?" they asked. "Have these men felt no pain?"

Feelings, vulnerability, pain? But look here, read there, don't you recognize . . . ? I felt both defensive and perplexed in the face of these critiques—defensive because I wanted these essays to "touch" and "move" readers; perplexed because I myself was moved by them and believed they were fraught with feelings. By way of personal conversation and letters, I knew the authors had written these stories not merely with conviction, but with feeling, sometimes passion. Certainly I undertook my own not just as an "interesting" project or an intellectual challenge, but as an exploration into the interior. I dreaded finding some harsh or disquieting truths that I knew were buried there, and I worried about how much to tell of what I found. At the end of my first draft I felt as if I had taken a pair of great risks: I had disclosed (or exposed?) myself; and I had used the language of novelists rather than academics, words that touch rather than dissect. Rereading the whole set of essays a fifteenth or perhaps thirtieth time, I continue to sense the surge of emotions in them. I feel with these men and for them.

Why, then, do readers tell me they find few feelings and almost no pain? Are we reading different essays? In one sense, we are. I read the current of emotion swirling beneath the surface of what is written. They read the surface that ripples with statement, analysis, and irony, with mistakes rather than vulnerabilities, anxieties rather than terror, injury rather than pain. Yes, reading over the shoulders of my readers, I understand their perspective. Compared to the testimonials and confessionals of women during the past ten years of their consciousness-raising movement, these essays hesitate. They put a hand on your shoulder instead of both arms wide around you.

And why is that?

WHY

First a personal statement. While writing this introduction I have struggled with a growing discomfort. How can I write fairly about a book that is my own project and in fact contains my own essay? Still more discomforting, how can I make assessments of essays written by my friends? The chances of bias are high. Worse, however, is the chance of violation. In generalizing about what these authors have written, I am afraid of deprecating and depersonalizing people who are my friends.

At first I chose to avoid these risks by avoiding any introduction at all. Let the essays speak for themselves! Eventually I decided that the essays needed an intermediary voice, like the narrator of *Our Town,* to point out themes and implications. My purpose in this essay-about-the-essays is neither to judge nor to vivisect these men's experiences. It is to understand their collective meanings and help our readers understand those meanings. I am writing here in a way that extends what I and my fellow authors have begun in our individual essays. Those are first-person-singular; this introduction shifts into first-person-plural and toward third-person-plural. But otherwise the intention is the same: to cope with those questions that Robert Hahn quotes from Gaugin, "Where Do We Come From, Who Are We, Where Are We Going?"

And I write these introductory pages with compassion because the best understanding needs compassion.

Growing Up Male

For convenience, let us begin with sexual stereotypes.[6] As social scientists have documented unmistakably, men form the master class in America. Men make the laws, control the economy, declare and fight the wars. America has been a maledom since the colonial beginnings and, until feminists win their campaign, it will continue to be a maledom. Privilege and power belong disproportionately to those who happen to have been born with a penis.

Mastery confers power and privilege, but it also makes demands. A man must earn mastery, first struggling out of the weakness of boyhood into the strengths of manhood, then struggling to win his place in the world of power. In subjective as well as objective dimensions, manhood is not simply an evolution, but an achievement. And as an achievement, it can be done well or badly. To become a man is to locate one's energies between the magnetic poles of success and failure, always flanked by those twin possibilities, always struggling. Even if (or perhaps especially if) a man succeeds greatly and earns his standing as a master, he must maintain it. The "earning" goes on relentlessly. When a body stands, the muscles flex with an effort that is hardly noticed unless the standing persists too long; only then does one recognize that standing is an act of will. In order not to fall, a man must hold on to his place and to himself. Control entails self-control. Power entails willpower against weakness.

This struggle may be offensive or defensive, but either way it pushes men into the realm of doing and out of the realm of feeling. According to the geography of sexual stereotypes, women stay at home amid children and feelings, while men work in the world of adults and forces and things. Women make people, literally in childbirth and figuratively in motherhood, wifehood, nursing, teaching, and other female activities. The product is really a process, a vital twine of feelings between her and others.

Many men also teach, heal, minister, and otherwise care for people, but as professionals, they are often required to put a "clinical distance" between them and their "clients." And often the rewards of the work compete for primacy with the work itself—hence, the brilliant physician who ends up in a laboratory working with projects rather than patients. And for a man outside of such professions, the emphasis is unmistakably nonpersonal. His computer or real estate or automobile chassis or blueprint forms a world of things, whether abstract or physical, rather than persons. In addition, the rules of success in this world call for him to put aside or put down all sorts of feelings. Timidity, spontaneity, playfulness, sympathy, generosity—any of these will impede him. A realtor should not feel sorry for his prospective customer; an electrical engineer should not turn whimsical. Emotions do not, after all, achieve or produce; they move, but do not make. And thus they interfere with the tasks of manhood, the task of making oneself into a man.

These stereotypes are just that—simplified, even simplistic, silhouettes. They describe man better than they describe individual men. Certainly they do not fit the men in this book. Tom Kreilkamp has learned, in the course of treating troubled families, to be specially aware of the importance of paternal caring, including his own caring for his own children. Steve Turner, as director of a technical-assistance organization on behalf of industrial workers, resented and resisted the bureaucratizing forces that came between him and the workers he wanted to help. Paul Fiddleman writes with horror about the technicians who refuse to see the bloody consequences of their research. And even while Harry Boyte was fighting his (nonviolent) war against white racism, he reached out for some basic brotherhood with a Klansman.

The men in this book have repudiated the stereotypes of manliness. As Arn Strasser puts it: ". . . to be willing to question the male prerogative, to share equally in housework and child raising, to be able to cry, to coddle, to mother, to be noncompetitive, to be gentle; these are qualities I will always strive for." I am gladdened by my fellow authors' efforts to live according to their own qualities and possibilities rather than according to a doctrinaire masculine script. But I think it fair to say that, even though we have repudiated the stereotypes, we have not yet escaped them. The generally cool and guarded style of the prose indicates that we are still stripping away the masculine armor. One sees the human flesh through the chinks between the metal. One sees the pain between the lines of prose.

Even more clearly than stylistic tone, the emphasis on work signals the incompleteness of our repudiation. None of us, except for Tom Kreilkamp, seems to have escaped John Calvin's hooks. These stories continually veer into work stories, as if the whole man can be found in that sphere of life. Does this inclination mean that men, even men who ostensibly want to go beyond stereotyped sex roles, are fooling themselves? No, I think that neither delusion nor hypocrisy explains what is going on. What then? Certain hypotheses have occured to me as I puzzled over the Calvinistic patterns of these autobiographies.

There is, first of all, a very pragmatic possibility: in trying to produce an interesting essay, one might find more to write—at least more that is easily written—if one focuses on occupational activities. Love, marriage, and parenthood are almost universal experiences, but an underground newspaper in Rhode Island or military service in Korea or dealing in Las Vegas are not. Would you rather see Andy Warhol's film of a man sleeping or his film about East Village hippies?

I also believe that writing about the exterior world is easier than writing about the interior. Here one might be tempted to return to the male-female stereotypes, claiming that men are unpracticed and uncomfortable with introspection. In fact, however, the contributors to this book are quite practiced and, presumably, quite comfortable. Several mention their experiences with psychotherapy, several have participated in men's consciousness-raising groups, and many hold dialogues with themselves through poetry, journals, or diaries. The interior experience is plentiful enough, but it is overshadowed on these pages by exterior experience because, I suspect, it resists easy transcription. A narrative of deeds seems more manageable than an expression of ideas and feelings.

In the end, however, these practical considerations seem to me only a part of the reason why these stories give primacy to work. The third, and probably weightiest, explanation is that we find more satisfaction and more self-definition in the occupational world. Certainly that is true of most American men. When a national sample of employed men were asked whether they would continue to hold a job if they inherited enough money to live comfortably without it, four out of five said they would keep on working.[7] More pointedly, a complex survey of several thousand middle-class men in the late 1950s concluded: "Work and leisure appear to be the two life situations that most strongly engage a man's interest. Marriage and parenthood are necessary for full adult status, but they act as supporting roles to what men see as the main theater for their behavior."[8] One finds the same conclusion in a thorough study of several thousand California men (both lower and middle class) who were interviewed periodically between their high school years in the 1930s and their adulthood in the 1960s. Men in both economic classes "valued work more highly than family life, leisure, or community roles."[9]

If men differ in their love of work, the difference comes not from economic class but from economic success. Upwardly mobile men consistently placed greater value upon their occupational role than did less successful men. Well, that fits common sense: the more rewards a man gets from his work, the more gladly he will invest his energies into it. The formula, however, has a darker side. At what price does he earn those rewards?

Earlier I mentioned a study that showed a direct correlation between success in career and deterioration in marital happiness. But the price extends further, into the man himself. In order to sustain the anxieties and pressures of succeeding—or let us say, of not failing—a man needs emotional support. Typically, he finds that support not among other men but among women, particularly his wife. He needs her to serve as the proverbial helpmate, the affirmer of his strengths and the consoler of his weaknesses. He needs her but cannot confess to needing her because confession exposes the vulnerability he is trying to deny. He has written a secret script of shameful dependence. Take notice that this is not simply the familiar story of wife's dependence upon husband, but also the less familiar story of husband's dependence upon wife. So say the psychologists at least.[10] What do the men in this book say?

A remarkable feature of these eight life stories, I think, is the prominence of wives. Although these men discuss work more than home and family, they nevertheless devote considerable, sometimes fervent, attention to spouses. At first glance that is no surprise. After all, they love their wives. Moreover, they have (or have learned) respect for them. Harry Boyte and Paul Fiddleman, for example, encouraged their wives' careers and boast of their accomplishments. Robert Hahn took over the household while his wife went to graduate school. Feminism has come home for these couples.

Love and respect are no surprise. But scattered phrases and episodes also betray a very different attitude: dependence. However these couples have turned out, many of them began quite otherwise. Robert Hahn "hurried" to be married, Paul Fiddleman "needed" to be married, and I proposed to Jeanette in "a panic" that she might go away. During Steve and Anne Turner's courtship, "both of us needed the constant reaffirmation of a supporting soul in attendance." When Marian had an affair and refused to continue her comforting role, Arn Strasser became frantic. Amid my doubts in graduate school, I craved my wife's reassurances but would neither confess the craving nor reveal the fragile "mystery" of my poetic self-image. Inside the armor beats a glass heart.

There may be a pattern of evolution here. As men grow into their thirties, their dependence diminishes or vanishes. In part this autonomy is the product of maturity. For some of us, it is also a by-product of having developed closer friendships with men. When the wives refused to serve as emotional crutches, the men found that they could walk on their own and, if they stumbled, could find support from another man's arm around the waist.

In terms of autonomy, then, these end up as success stories. But we should not let this rosy statement blind us to some less rosy facts about the earlier phases. Pushed or pulled to achieve and succeed, these men spent many years off balance, needing wifely support but—loyal to manly teachings—hesitating to ask openly for it. A double bind. If women often are trapped in passivity or domesticity by the "fear of success," their co-stars in the drama of the sexes thrash (silently) in a no less binding trap.

Another such mirror image has occurred to me as I contemplated these stories. During early adulthood, many of the authors needed time in which to postpone career choices. Some of us took that time, whether by short-run jobs, military service, or resolute "hippie" rejection of career. Others did not take that time, because they didn't want it or because they couldn't afford it. In all cases, however, they were choosing among a set of occupational roles, seeking the least inhibiting possibility until a true calling emerged. Suppose, however, that during this interim "search period" these men could have "gone home" and been househusbands. Suppose that, temporarily, they could have had the satisfaction of domestic achievements: delicious meals, loving spouse, happy children. Or if not these achievements, suppose they at least had had time free from money earning in which to discover or test their vocational interests. It is significant, I think, that those authors who did play strong family roles seemed to have had an extra source of security. Arn Strasser in his commune and Harry Boyte in his fifty-fifty parenthood found a time and also a place in which to ready themselves for their eventual vocation. Tom Kreilkamp, indeed, wishes to stay home more than half of every week, and only financial necessity and his wife's resistance stand in his way.[11]

Mirror logic opens up unexpected angles of vision. Without denying that women have been oppressed by men and by their socialization into "femininity," I would add that men are in many ways victimized by themselves and by their socialization into "masculinity." The eight in this book are struggling along various routes to escape the confines and become more fully themselves.

But strangely enough, none of us mentions one escape route: homosexuality or bisexuality. The most determined, and also most publicized, resistance to the "masculine mystique" has been by gay men. Until the 1970s, American homosexuals had led a marginal, often secretive and shamed existence. To be open about their sexual preference meant to risk ridicule, blackmail, or loss of job. But in 1969 a symbolic event took place. When New York City policemen raided a popular gay male bar in Greenwich Village, the patrons did not respond as they had to the many previous raids. Instead of sullen compliance, they fought back with bricks and trashcans. The episode turned out to be the first shot of the "gay revolution." A decade later, innumerable men have come "out of the closet" to admit their homosexuality, and even more innumerable others—especially among those aged twenty to thirty-five—have engaged in bisexual activity. Yet none of these developments are echoed in the pages of these eight essays. In one respect, this is a regrettable omission. Other men's anthologies give attention to homosexual experience, while ours ends up exclusively heterosexual. In another respect, however, this omission says something significant about our particular age cohort. A small minority of men born in the 1930s and 1940s engaged at least temporarily in homosexual activity, but they were relatively few and they were distinctly deviant. As Paul Fiddleman remarks in the "Afterwords" section: "to us of the 1950s, any recognition, let alone admission, of homosexual urges would have scared the living shit out of us." Only among those ten or twenty years younger did alternatives to heterosexuality become first a defiant assertion of "rights," and then increasingly a quiet option of "life style." The authors of this book may belong to the last "generation" for whom heterosexuality is an almost automatic presumption.[12]

Although traditional about sexual behavior, the essays are un-traditional about other parts of masculinity. How many of the seventy-five million American adult males do these eight represent? No one knows and I would not guess. Certainly there is no men's movement comparable in size or self-definition to the women's movement. The most visible, organized, and purposeful organizations are those that agitate on behalf of "gay rights." Like other minority groups, gay persons have definable oppressors—discriminatory landlords, employers, publications, laws, etc.—and therefore a well-defined agenda seeking equality of treatment. Outside of gay rights, however, the agenda of men's liberation turns hazy. It is hard to show how the masters are oppressed. "We are," says one proponent, "the-not-quite-ready-for-prime-time revolution." If not an on-going movement, however, there is certainly a scattered male chorus "out there" echoing many of the themes in this book. The five National Conferences on Men and Masculinity during 1975–1978 (the last one in Los Angeles with 600 persons attending) testify to that.[13] And so does the steadily swelling stream of books, journals, and articles about men's roles and male identity.[14] The writings and conferences and agitation all turn the question of "why" in a second direction: not psychological history, but collective history.

Growing Up
Since The 1930s

As boys, we were no different from other middle-class boys of the post-World War II era. Our life stories rehearse the cultural clichés: Mickey Mantle; Davy Crockett; afternoons of shooting baskets or playing war; fantasies of Brigitte Bardot; forbidding fathers and indulgent mothers; perhaps some guilt about the plight of less privileged coutrymen; and an irresistible, unchosen momentum into college.

Poised on the brink of adulthood in the late 1950s or early 1960s, we were a historical type. The reasonable, respectful, and lavishly attentive child rearing of Dr. Spock lay behind us—so attentive that many of us felt "special." Prosperity, patriotism, and complacency lay comfortably around us, although some of us made rude noises in the name of the poor, the blacks, or world peace. Ahead of us lay a future full of promise, and we spelled out the promise as our culture had taught us; we would "have" a professional career, a loving wife, and of course several children. In other words, we emerged from boyhood with a conventionally "masculine" sense of identity, with a sense of success, and with expectations of achieving a conventional, still more successful manhood. How, then, did we come to be authors of essays in which we question the meaning of "success" and applaud the revision of sex roles?

One explanation derives from our very masculinization. Boys who develop a strong and sure sense of their gender identity are more likely to feel the self-confidence enabling them to modify that identity. They have been so well trained and armed to compete in the masculine arena that they feel secure enough to disarm themselves if some "nonmasculine" alternatives seem more attractive.[15] But why did alternatives appear for these young men and not for earlier generations of no less socialized men? This psychological explanation is, as philosophers say, necessary but not sufficient. It does not tell us what in particular—in the particularity of their experiences—happened to make the difference for these young men. In order to make that particular (sufficient) explanation, we must look at American history of the 1960s. During that decade, two sets of events undermined many men's commitment to their conventional role. One set occurred among men themselves, the other occurred among women.

When four black freshmen at North Carolina Agricultural and Technical College sat down for a cup of coffee at a segregated lunch counter in 1960, the civil rights movement began. When one thousand students at the University of California, Berkeley, sat down in the foyers and offices of Sproul Hall in 1964, the student movement began. When Lyndon Johnson bombed North Vietnam in 1965, the peace movement began. And at some time that has no date of birth, a counterculture emerged among the younger generation, bearing names like acid and grass, hippie and dropout, coalescing in brief spectacles like Woodstock and Haight-Ashbury, and continually vibrating the atmosphere with the brash beat of its music.

This dissident history, I should quickly point out, was directly experienced only by some Americans. Most saw it on television, either watching with the same disinterest they gave to any other nightly program, or watching with contemptuous anger. For only a small minority of Americans, most of them in their teens and twenties, was the radical history of the 1960s also a personal experience. Such was the case for half of the men in this book. They marched, picketed, leafleted, and went to jail; they defied their parents, teachers, and peers; and one day they realized that they had somehow become a rebel, an outsider—call it what you will— but in any case someone other than they had expected to become during the mellow 1950s.

Radicalization—that is a familiar story, and it is not the one I am telling here. The story of this book is gender, and the question is how the radical social movements of the 1960s affected these men's definition of themselves as men. For Arn Strasser, the effect is unmistakable. Having entered Michigan State University to become a hard-working, affluent businessman, he emerged from the antiwar movement as an enemy of materialism, competition, violence, and alienating work. In short, his radical philosophy revoked most of the masculine values that he had been taught. His parents could hardly recognize the son they had raised. In the south, meanwhile, Harry Boyte was going through the crucible of the civil rights movement, first as the protégé of his father but gradually as his father's rival. Instead of emulating the solitary, impervious, strong and silent revolutionary image, Boyte questioned it. He began to fear the appetite of power, began to nourish sharing, modesty, love.

These two men exemplify—in highly exaggerated form, of course—certain tendencies among many other men of their generation.[16] By the early 1970s, the New Left and the counterculture had disintegrated. But their reverberations lived on, influencing men's attitudes about work and family.

Although a vast majority of high school and college students in 1968–1971 told pollsters they felt a commitment to hard work and a career, a rapidly growing number of them objected to being "bossed around" on the job. They valued "freedom to make my own decisions" and "work that seems important to me." By the mid-1970s, those values were exerting impact on business corporations, law firms, factories, and other fortresses of the work ethic.

According to an American Management Association survey in 1973, four out of five businessmen and corporation executives said their attitudes toward achievement and success were changing. They located their basic aspirations not in the companies that employed them, but in their families and private lives. Toward the lower end of the occupational ladder, dissatisfaction also mounted. The "blue-collar blues," or some said a "blue-collar revolt," spread particularly among younger workers. When asked what they wanted from their jobs, higher pay and security were halfway down their list; first came "interesting work." Throughout the work world, employers have been encountering a new spirit among their employees. "There's something different about the new generation that we're hiring," declared the division head of a large midwestern architectural firm. A vice-president of United Auto Workers echoed him: "People look at life in different ways than they used to. Maybe we ought to stop talking about the work ethic and start talking about the life ethic."[17]

The extent of this swerve in work attitudes will remain unclear until more time permits more perspective. The extent to which these attitudes can be put into practice is even more difficult to assess. "Flextime" (flexible work schedules), paternity leaves, sabbaticals for businessmen, job sharing by two people or even two spouses—all these devices have begun to ease the pressure of "John Calvin's hooks."[18] But for the vast majority of men, especially those outside of professions, work still has them as much as they have work.

The social upheavals of the 1960s may have sent seismic cracks through men's notions of their work role; the causality is arguable and the effects are not yet in. But there is no argument at all about another effect of the 1960s history. Out of the New Left was born the feminist movement which, in turn, has sent shock wave after shock wave through the heads, hearts, and power of men. To an unprecedented extent, women made men's history in the 1970s.

"Sara's attendance [at women's meetings] made me anxious . . ." Harry Boyte recalls. "Would she discover secret angers? . . . Would Sara's widening circle of women friends damage the closeness of our relationship?" This is how almost all men responded when "their" women developed feminist ideas and attachments. No matter whether they were committed to the status quo or, like

Boyte, committed to changing it, men felt threatened by the women's movement. Indeed, radical men felt a particularly keen threat because they were caught in a devastating crunch between their principles and practices. On the one hand, they preached equality for the poor, blacks, and other underprivileged classes. On the other hand, they wittingly or unwittingly practiced sexual inequality. In their New Left organizations, men chaired the meetings, gave the speeches, and made the decisions, while women more often than not were voting for the decisions applauding the speeches, running the mimeograph machines, making the coffee, and going to bed with the men who asked. When some of the women pointed out the inconsistency here, and called for equality of gender as well as economics and race, the men felt surprised, threatened, hostile, almost panicky. By 1967, a group of angry feminists walked out of the male New Left, forming a movement for themselves and other women.

They joined a current already swirling with the agitations of Betty Friedan. She had written the best-selling *Feminine Mystique* in 1963, urging women to take their educations and energies out of stultifying housekeeping and motherhood, into a job or career. Three years later, wanting to put her words into action, she formed the National Organization for Women to fight against sex discrimination on legal and economic fronts.[19]

By 1970, few Americans could have been unaware that a feminist movement was surging through their society. They saw it in the raised fists of ten thousand women marching down New York's Fifth Avenue. They saw it in the stern face of Kate Millett staring at them from the cover of *Time* magazine. They watched it erupt in not-so-funny arguments between Gloria, with newly raised consciousness, and her liberal husband Michael and arch-conservative father Archie Bunker. When feminism entered the popular television show *All in the Family,* it entered the living rooms of millions of Americans.

It entered more immediately, too: in the form of new, loud, disturbing statements by wives to husbands. "Pick up your own dirty socks." "Don't you dare laugh at me." "But I don't *care* if you want to make love now." "I'm going to get a job." As women demanded or made changes in their half of the relationships, men had to respond. When one person shifts on the seesaw, the other must move, or jump off.

All of the men in this book moved toward equality of roles. Harry Boyte not only discovered that cooking was more enjoyable than washing dishes, but found enormous gratification as parent to his son. Starting with a traditional division of roles, Paul Fiddleman and his wife entered negotiations about grocery shopping, baby sitting, and other duties, until finally—with his exuberant support—she entered nursing school and then a full-time career. "My wife is a liberated woman and I'm only a partly liberated man," Lawrence Rubin says, but with much struggle he has found a (sometimes shaky) balance between his occupational and his domestic responsibilities. In my own case, after a ten-year marriage in which I did none of the cooking and almost none of the child rearing, I finally discovered the joys I had been missing: the joys of kneading and shaping bread, of baking lasagne, of playing with my children. I also learned a more general satisfaction when, in my second marriage, I shed (or tried to shed) the burden of power and thereby gave myself more room for feelings and activities that are not masterful, not responsible, but mine. Robert Hahn sums it up deftly:

> Finding a way to solve (at least in our own lives) the societal problem of sexism has proved to be one of the best experiences of my life, and it has gone far—along with the shared sense of humor and the general camaraderie—toward making sense of this strange legal arrangement called marriage.

And what about the rest of American couples? Unless people open the doors of their lives and allow us to look in as these authors have done, we can only surmise what is happening in their relationships. Certainly the days of patriarchy are gone among middle-class families—have been gone for decades, in fact. Familial democracy became the middle-class ideal by the 1940s or even earlier. It did not become practice, however, except among a minority of families and with respect to certain sorts of domestic activities. Seventy-five percent of husbands did no more than "help out" on "female" chores such as cooking, cleaning, and child care. On the average, Mr. America gave two hours per day to housework, while Mrs. America gave (if employed) twice or (if not employed) four times that amount. Equally telling is the fact that the large majority of children turned to Mom for affection, guidance, and day-to-day supervision. Father may have ceased to be patriarch, but he remained a largely absentee authority. Between principle and practice fell the shadow of inconsistency.[20]

Despite the surge of feminism, that shadow shrank only slightly during the 1970s. More wives, and even more mothers, are employed than ever before, especially in the middle class, and yet they receive little more household help from their husbands than nonemployed wives receive. The so-called two-career family is really a two-and-a-half-career family, because the wife carries more than her half of household responsibilities. Don't lay all the blame on lazy husbands, however. According to a national sample of American households in the early 1970s, only one fifth of women said they wanted more help from their spouses. Traditional sex-role teachings have etched their mark on both sexes.[21]

General averages, though, camouflage some striking changes among particular groups of Americans. Younger, college-educated people are diverging sharply from their parents' idea of how to be male or female. According to a survey of college freshmen in 1970, for example, one half of the men and one third of the women agreed that "the activities of married women are best confined to the home and family." Five years later, the rate of agreement had plummeted by 60 percent. In 1977, yet another poll asked a sample of Americans whether they preferred the idea of shared marriage roles or a "traditional" marriage. Among the general population, shared roles emerged the slight but surprising winner, 48 to 43 percent; among persons aged eighteen to twenty-nine, however, it won by the emphatic margin of three to one. The last piece of evidence comes from a survey of 28,000 readers of *Psychology Today,* a group who are younger, more educated, and more affluent than most Americans. The responses point toward an androgynous culture. Most of the men want to be warmer, gentler, more loving, and they disdain competition, aggressiveness, or sexual conquest. Most of the women, in turn, share the same ideals for men and for themselves.[22]

What does it all add up to? The contemporary feminist movement seems likely to be the most far-reaching and enduring of the three American women's rights movements during the past century and a half.[23] But the consequences thus far have touched women more than men. To most Americans, it triggers classic defensive images of "a war between the sexes" such as James Thurber portrayed in his moody cartoons. Only a minority of people, male or female, interpret feminism positively as a step toward sexual equality, much less toward male liberation. But most Americans are not all Americans. If one looks at people in their twenties and thirties, especially those with college educations and in professions, the prognosis looks quite different. In vivid contrast to those Thurber drawings, a cartoon in *Playboy*—yes, *Playboy!*—portrayed that familiar ninety-pound weakling and his girl and the bully on the beach, but this time the weakling (in sandals) is kicking the sand, saying, "Get lost, creep! There's a new man on the beach and your macho bullshit doesn't cut it anymore!" And the bully replies, "That man is the biggest nuisance on the beach! Why can't he learn that *real* men today are gentle and sensitive and. . . ." Meanwhile, the girlfriend murmurs to herself, "This is getting a little weird. . . ."[24]

I offer one other conclusion. Ten years of feminist accomplishment, even extraordinary accomplishment, is hardly a moment if one is considering basic cultural change. And sex roles are among the most basic parts of any culture. To measure change in sex roles, one must use a clock marked not in years, but in decades. However quickly the angry feminists march and however speedily they pass the laws or obtain jobs for women, collective behavior and attitudes evolve slowly, very slowly.

Growing Into Middle Age

There is collective historical time, and there is also personal historical time. The men in this book have been influenced by events happening around and to them since World War II. We have also participated in another sort of history, which is the cycle of our personal development. All of us passed through childhood, when we learned how to grow up male. But growing up is an on-going process, not a destination, and childhood is simply the first of several stages of development, each of them bringing its own significant consequences. Probably the most consequential is the midlife stage, which is the one that we—aged thirty-six to forty-four—are entering or completing. We live in a stormy solstice, looking back at what we have achieved and foregone during the first half of life, looking ahead to what we may hope for or must settle for.

We are men in the middle. We are men in the middle of not merely one transition, but two: the societal revision of conventional sex roles, and also the personal revision of ourselves.

Until the 1960s, psychologists virtually ignored middle age in men, presuming that it signaled the end of personal development and the onset of declining capacities. If there was any interior history, they supposed it to be a defensive one: either frustration, panic, or growing resignation on the slick slope toward death. Significant male development, they assumed, occurred before the age of forty (or, some orthodox Freudians argued, before the age of eight). This perspective has reminded one scholar of an anecdote about Stalin's son, who said to his mother shortly before the Russian Revolution: "Father should get out and do something; all he does is walk in the park with Lenin."[25]

After the work of Erik Erikson began to appear in the 1950s, however, this short-run view seemed increasingly fallacious. According to Erikson's theory of eight life stages, personal identity continues to evolve long after the Oedipal crisis—indeed, as long as a person's lifetime. "Identity" and "growth" quickly came to the fore of the psychological profession, especially the wing known as "humanistic psychology." Meanwhile, therapists, journalists, and even novelists turned "the male midlife crisis" into a familiar slogan. In 1978 this trend received its most articulate certification with the publication of Daniel J. Levinson's *The Seasons of a Man's Life*, which synthesizes a ten-year team-research project on adult male development. By now, who can doubt that there is indeed life after forty?[26]

Precisely what kind of life, however, depends on how a man navigates the transition between his fourth and fifth decades. This period, Levinson claims, need not always be a crisis. Some men arrive at the end of it having undergone little tumult or trauma. But that is not the case for most. In fact, it cannot be the case, says Levinson, unless a man willfully shuts his mind against the profound questions that arise during this phase. And it *should* not be the case, because those questions need answering; refusal to answer will simply postpone the crisis or, worse, produce "a progressive withering of the self and a life structure minimally connected to the self." Questioning will be painful but, Levinson insists, it is not a sign of sickness. On the contrary, it "stems from the most healthy part of the self," expressing a man's efforts to work his way productively through a profound reappraisal of where he has been and where he is going. In Levinson's view, the years between thirty-eight and forty-three link two "seasons" of male development, forming a natural, inherently turbulent, and consequential transition.

What is being reappraised? Virtually every part of the "life structure" that a man has built. The two most salient parts are his sense of success in work and his satisfaction with marriage and parenthood. By the age of thirty-eight or thirty-nine, the "returns are in," one might say. A man knows how much or little he is likely to achieve of his youthful dreams of money, fame, or power; he is deeply involved in familial patterns and responsibilities; he has "become his own man" and now must step back and look at who that man is.

But beneath the realms of work and family lie more general issues, which Levinson formulates as four polarities with which the midlife man must come to terms. *Young/Old:* no longer younger but not yet old, he must acknowledge his "in-betweenness" and prepare for growing older. *Destruction/Creation:* correspondingly he must experience the mortality of loved ones as well as himself, but at the same time he needs to give room and voice to creative urges that he has deferred or not even recognized. *Separation/Attachment:* during this time he becomes aware of the ways he has ignored people, set himself against them, hurt them; more positively, he feels a desire to contribute to human welfare. *Masculine/Feminine:* these inclinations toward creativity and attachment belong to his fourth "task," which is to integrate more fully the "feminine" aspects of his personality.

After almost forty years of making choices in order to build a life structure that is as fulfilling as possible, a man must confront the options he chose against, the desires he chose to subordinate, the other voices in other rooms of his self. And at the end of this second look and new listening, he will have formed the basis— whether a stable or unstable basis—for the structure of the rest of his life. As Levinson puts it, he will have performed a process of "individuation," a painstaking and painful redefinition of who he is.[27]

Although Levinson's interpretation of midlife seems to me the most articulate and persuasive thus far, it is certainly not the last word. Rather, it serves as a useful map for other researchers in this underexplored field of male psychology. They must gather more evidence about more men (and also women) to test Levinson's claims; after all, his team worked with a sample of only forty individuals. More basically, researchers must assess his theory of "seasons"—a succession of invariable and necessary phases of growth. Dissenting psychologists argue that seasons are really psycho-social stages triggered by external events and therefore developing in no fixed sequence and at no fixed ages.[28]

Whatever the ultimate fate of Levinson's interpretation, how well does it illuminate a "figure in the carpet" of the life stories in this book? For half of us, remarkably well. At the age of thirty-nine—the age that Jack Benny refused to grow beyond—Robert Hahn drew a line and stepped across it. Renouncing the anarchic childlike emotions of his "shadow life" as a poet, and bored with his career as a teacher, he entered a graduate program in educational administration. "I understood that I needed the conventional certainties and supports of a profession, a position. This, apparently, was who I was. The recognition was refreshing."

At the age of thirty-seven, Steve Turner abruptly stepped out from behind his desk, resigned his administrative job, left Boston, and began to enact his college-days dream of professional writing. Living amid the Massachusetts countryside, he hoped to find the freedom "for a new period of reconsideration about work and about family."

At the age of thirty-eight, I wrote a happy ending to my essay. At the age of thirty-nine I tore it up because it no longer fit me, if indeed it ever fit. As though set off punctually by Daniel Levinson's midlife alarm clock, my work and my marriage exploded with results that I do not yet know how to name.

For Paul Fiddleman, who was born in 1934 and is the oldest contributor, no ninety-degree turn or volcanic eruption marked his journey past the Jack Benny age. Gone are the dreams of laying Brigitte Bardot and making a million bucks, but they seem to have left quietly. If he has "gone over the hump" so smoothly, however, was it a genuine midlife transition at all? Or is Fiddleman (himself a psychologist) simply imposing the "proper" label? I believe it was a transition, but not with the fanfare described by others in this book. I find Fiddleman's transition not in any actions related by the essay, but in the very action of writing the essay. While looking back, he catches up with the meaning of where he has come. "These last few paragraphs have helped clarify something that has bothered me for years," he writes. For years he had been visiting his parents and returning with a vague sense that "something was missing." Midway through the essay he penetrates the vagueness: "I had been looking for the thread that hangs all this [life of mine] together, the 'why,' the game plan. Now I realize there never was any. . . ." This discovery, in turn forms the theme for his future: "There's more coming, a lot of crossroads and choice points." The end of his essay marks the end of his transition.

These four life stories move in the seasonal rhythm predicted by Levinson's theory. Not so for others, however. In the case of Harry Boyte and Arn Strasser, the reason may be that they had not yet reached the critical age of thirty-eight when they wrote their essays. Ask them for a postscript a few years hence, and perhaps each will provide an "orthodox" midlife crisis. Yes, a crisis— but I wonder whether it will follow the pattern that Levinson lays down. He claims that men must come to terms with the masculine choices they have made thus far: competition, individualism, power or money, subordination of feelings and family. But Strasser and Boyte have already renounced those values. Indeed, Strasser rejected the idea of a career throughout his twenties, the decade which usually serves as a man's entrée to his work identity. At the age of thirty-four, he began his chiropractic career ten years "late," just as his remarriage and second child have come "late." If or when these two men undergo a midlife reappraisal, will they move toward the "masculine" half of Levinson's polarities? Or as a result of having already integrated their "feminine" halves more fully into their lives, will they have built a more balanced and complete "life structure" and therefore have less need for violent reconstruction?

The pattern of "lateness" also characterizes Lawrence Rubin's biography. He too had no career in his twenties, though less for ideological than for psychological reasons. In addition, unlike either Boyte or Strasser he remained unmarried. Those choices came in his early thirties, and the choice of parenthood ten years after that. When we find no hint of midlife upheaval in his essay, written when he was forty and "should be" in upheaval, what do we make of the silence? Perhaps a contradiction to psychologists' theory of male development. Or perhaps a refinement, this time not because Rubin has renounced conventional masculine values, but because he has revised conventional phasing of masculine career and family.

Finally there is Tom Kreilkamp, the fourth essayist without midlife crisis. To be sure, he was only thirty-seven when he wrote his story. Given what he writes, however, I cannot imagine what his midlife crisis would entail. He has long ago renounced success and even ambition, has happily taken on his role as husband and parent, and looks forward to spending at least part of every week writing and reading at home. Whereas T. S. Eliot prayed "Teach me to care and not to care, teach me to sit still," Kreilkamp seems to have learned how to do that. His essay bristles with "problems," but it contains not a whisper of anything like "crisis." Maybe his forties will surprise him, as midlife seems to have a way of doing. Maybe, like me, he will have to tear up his last pages. But I wouldn't bet on that.

CONCLUSION

I will not develop a finale with grand extended Beethovenesque passages. After so many words from me, it is time—long overdue time—for you to hear from the other men who have made this book.

More important, these essays permit no finale. As the title announces, we are in midpassage, and can only guess our destinations. We are living in the middle of our personal histories. Less obviously, we are also in the middle of a collective American history in which the established configuration of sexual roles is shifting, cracking, glacially yielding to a different configuration. For women, the movement has been occurring long enough that one can discuss it confidently. For men, the movement is so incipient that one wonders, sometimes, if one is hearing the sounds of actual change or merely the echoes of women's voices, or simply the murmurs of dreams.

We make no clarion call. We trumpet no phalanx of male liberationists into a (nonviolent) battle, proclaim no triumph. It is too soon for trumpets and triumph. Our life stories enact the struggle rather than recount it. They form another set of voices to join in that scattered male chorus which, perhaps, will eventually acquire the solidarity and, most of all, the analytic clarity of the women's movement. But it is too soon to say anything so final.

NOTES

1. Sara Ruddick and Pamela Daniels, ed., *Working It Out* (New York, 1977).
2. Harold L. Wilensky, "The Uneven Distribution of Leisure: The Impact of Economic Growth on 'Free Time'," *Social Problems*, IX (Summer, 1961), reprinted in *Work and Leisure: A Contemporary Social Problem,*ed. Erwin O. Smigel (New Haven, Conn., 1963), pp. 116–123. Also William H. Whyte, *The Organization Man* (New York, 1956), p. 144.
3. Jan E. Dizard, "The Price of Success," in *The Future of the Family*, ed. Louise Kapp Howe (New York, 1972), pp. 194–197.
4. According to a U.S. Bureau of Labor Statistics study, "Occupational Mobility of Workers" (1979), 11.5 percent of employed men and women changed occupations in 1977, as compared to 9 percent five years earlier. A study by the National Institute of Education claims that one-third of the adult population is in "career transition." More of them are women than men, and most are motivated by financial need. The average age is thirty-eight. For these data, see Nancy Rubin, "Midlife Changes Become a Way of Life," *New York Times*, October 14, 1979. More generally, see Seymour B. Sarason, *Work, Aging and Social Change: Professionals and the One Life–One Career Imperative* (New York, 1977), esp. ch. XI. For oblique references, see Seymour Spilerman, "Careers, Labor Market Structure, and Socioeconomic Achievement," *American Journal of Sociology*, 83 (November 1977), 551–593; Richard L. Simpson and David R. Norsworth, "The Changing Occupational Structure of the South," in *The South in Continuity and Change*, eds. John C. McKinney and Edgar T. Thompson (Durham, N.C., 1965); and Glen H. Elder, Jr., *Children of the Great Depression: Social Change in Life Experience* (Chicago, 1974), Table A–21, p. 213. I am grateful to Richard L. Simpson for help on this topic.
5. Elizabeth Douvan and Joseph Adelson, *The Adolescent Experience* (New York, 1966); see also notes 7, 8, and 9 below.
6. Among the voluminous literature on sex-typing, I have benefited most from Ruth E. Hartley, "Sex-role Pressures in the Socialization of the Male Child," *Psychological Reports*, V (1959), 457–568, reprinted in *Men and Masculinity*, ed. Joseph H. Pleck and Jack Sawyer (Englewood Cliffs, N.J., 1974); Jean Baker Miller, *Toward a New Psychology of Women* (Boston, 1976); Warren Farrell, *The Liberated Man* (New York, 1974), esp. ch. 3; Deborah David and Robert Brannon, ed., *The Forty-Nine Percent Majority* (Reading, Mass., 1976); and two articles in a special issue about male roles, Michael V. Cicone and Diane N. Ruble, "Beliefs about Males," and Robert A. Lewis, "Emotional Intimacy among Men," *The Journal of Social Issues*, XXXIV, No. 1, (1978), 5–16, 108–121.
7. Nancy S. Morse and Robert S. Weiss, "The Function and Meaning of Work and the Job," *American Sociological Review*, XX (April 1955), 191–198.

8. Joseph Veroff and Sheila Feld, *Marriage and Work in America: A Study of Motives and Roles* (New York, 1970), pp. 337–338.

9. Elder, *Children of the Great Depression*, p. 186.

10. Miller, *Toward a New Psychology of Women*, pp. 31–33.

11. For a particularly honest confrontation, see Paul Cowan, "Can Men Really Be Feminists?" *Village Voice*, February 17, 1975, 33. Also, S. M. Miller, "The Making of a Confused, Middle-Aged Husband," *Social Policy*, II (July–August 1971), 33–39, reprinted in Pleck and Sawyer, *Men and Masculinity*, pp. 44–52; David Steinberg, "Redefining Fatherhood," in *The Future of the Family*, ed. Howe, pp. 368–378.

12. On incidence of homosexuality in the 1940s and in the early 1970s, see Alfred Kinsey, *Sexual Behavior in the Human Male* (Philadelphia, 1948), pp. 650–651, and Morton Hunt, *Sexual Behavior in the 1970s* (New York, Dell edn., 1975), pp. 303–319. For exemplary anthologies, see Karla Jay and Allen Young, eds., *After You're Out: Personal Experiences of Gay Men and Lesbian Women* (New York, 1978); Nancy and Casey Adair, *Word Is Out: Stories of Some of Our Lives* (New York, 1978).

13. Perry Garfinkel, "The Men's Movement," *The Real Paper* (Boston), January 20, 1979, pp. 14–20 (the quotation is from Bob Brannon). Also, Carol Kleiman, " 'Good-bye, John Wayne'? Three Days at a Men's Conference," *Ms.* (April 1978), 45–47, 77.

14. Outstanding examples include Pleck and Sawyer, ed., *Men and Masculinity;* Farrell, *Liberated Man;* Phyllis Chesler, *About Men* (New York, 1978); Herb Goldberg, *The Hazards of Being Male: Surviving the Myth of Masculine Privilege* (New York, 1976). For bibliography, see James B. Harrison, "Men's Roles and Men's Lives," *Signs*, IV, No. 2 (Winter 1979), 324–336; Carol Tavris, "Is This 'The Year of the Man'?" *Ms.* (April 1978), 51, 78; Bibliography of the Men's Studies Collection, Massachusetts Institute of Technology.

15. Virginia E. O'Leary and James M. Donoghue, "Latitudes of Masculinity," *Journal of Social Issues*, XXXIV, No. 1 (1978), 17–28.

16. For a fuller analysis, see Peter G. Filene, *Him/Her/Self: Sex Roles in Modern America* (New York, 1975), pp. 211–220.

17. For polls, blue-collar attitudes, and other information, see Daniel Yankelovich, *The New Morality: A Profile of American Youth in the 70s* (New York, 1974), ch. 10 and *passim; Work in America: Report of a Special Task Force to the Secretary of Health, Education and Welfare* (Cambridge, Mass., 1973), pp. 29–38, 43–51. The UAW quotation is from *Time* (October 30, 1972), 96–97. American Management Association poll is in *New York Times*, June 3, 1973, IV, 12. For the architect's quotation and general analysis of young executives, see Louis Banks, "Here Come the Individualists," *Harvard Magazine* (September–October, 1977), 24–29. For a complex typology of motivations, based on a survey of 8,000 business school graduates, see Barry Liebling, "Beyond Work Stereotypes," *MBA*, XII (August–September, 1978), 13–25.

18. For example, Farrell, *Liberated Man*, ch. 8; *Work in America*, ch. 4; Edward Lawler, "Workers Can Set Their Own Wages Responsibly," *Psychology To-*

day (February 1977), 109–112; publications by New Ways to Work, 457 Kingsley Avenue, Palo Alto, CA, 94301.

19. For the full story, see Sara Evans, *Personal Politics* (New York, 1979); also Judith Hole and Ellen Levine, *Rebirth of Feminism* (New York, 1971).

20. On household roles, see William H. Chafe, *The American Woman: Her Changing Social, Economic and Political Roles, 1920–1970* (New York, 1972), pp. 221–225. On housework times, Irene H. Frieze et al., ed. *Women and Sex Roles: A Social Psychological Perspective* (New York, 1978), pp. 143–145; Carol Tavris and Carole Offir, *The Longest War: Sex Differences in Perspective* (New York, 1977), pp. 230–232. On familial democracy, see Filene, *Him/Her/Self*, pp. 197–202, and for further sources, see pp. 329–332, notes 44–47.

21. Tavris and Offir, *Longest War*, pp. 230–232.

22. William H. Chafe, *Women and Equality* (New: York, 1977), p. 139; *New York Times*, November 27, 1977, 75; Carol Tavris, "Men and Women Report Their Views on Masculinity," *Psychology Today*, X (January 1977), 35–42, 87.

23. Chafe, *Women and Equality*, ch. 6.

24. *Playboy*, XXI (September 1974), 147. Also see the accompanying article by Richard Woodley, "We Have Seen the Enemy and He Is Us," pp. 151, 212.

25. Orville G. Brim, Jr., "Theories of the Male Mid-Life Crisis," *Counseling Psychologist*, VI, No. 1 (1976), 2. I am grateful to Judith Kuspit for calling my attention to this article and others.

26. Erik Erikson, *Childhood and Society*, 2nd edn. (New York, 1963), esp. pp. 247–274; Erikson, "Identity and the Life Cycle," *Psychological Issues*, I (1950), 1–171; Daniel J. Levinson, et al., *The Seasons of a Man's Life* (New York, 1978); George E. Vaillant, *Adaptation to Life* (Boston, 1977). Among the more thoughtful popularizing accounts, see Roger Gould, *Transformations: Growth and Change in Adult Life* (New York, 1978), and Nancy Mayer, *The Male Mid-Life Crisis: Fresh Starts after Forty* (New York, 1978). For bibliographical reviews, see Brim, "Theories of the Male Mid-Life Crisis" and Daniel Sinick, "Mini-Reviews of Books on Mid-Life," *Counseling Psychologist*, VI, No. 1 (1976), 8–9, 68–70. Two recent novels are Joseph Heller, *Good as Gold* (New York, 1979), and Philip F. O'Connor, *Stealing Home* (New York, 1979).

27. Levinson, *Seasons*, esp. pp. 196–199.

28. Brim, "Theories," 7.

2
In Movement

by Harry C. Boyte

When I was eight or nine I stopped crying, for what I thought would be forever. Crying seemed unbecoming for a general. I was in charge of an army which drilled endlessly in our back-yard and had a hideout in the branches and leaves on top of the garage.

My first officer, Sharon, held the rank because she told me that an arch-rival of mine had become her best boyfriend. I promoted her and she reinstated me. Our relationship had a kind of rough symmetry. My sister, Anne, was also an officer, as was Sharon's younger brother, Wright. The number of privates, varying, was sufficient to spark neighborhood outrage when we changed the trashcan tops into shields.

One day we went on an expedition across the tops of things—trees, houses, fences, garages, greenhouses. I crashed through the greenhouse, slicing open my chest. Then in full view of the rest of the army, I pulled myself out of the tomato plants, dripping blood, and marched home.

Talk of my slow and steady trek spread through the children's underground. I kept the bloodied shirt hidden in my drawer to show everyone for weeks, until my mother noticed the smell. Recruitment for our army picked up. My father made up a ballad to the tune of "Davy, Davy Crockett," which envisioned great things for my future. My mother fainted when the doctor removed the stitches. And I, swelling with pride, decided that the key to my success was my fearless, tearless insouciance.

I was modeling myself a lot on my father, for whom a kind of Olympian indifference toward the world's opinions was a constant pose and toward whom I felt, to put it mildly, ambivalence. Underneath he felt scared of being different, I came to realize much later. But at the time, what struck me most dramatically was his studied nonchalance coupled with his own rebellious career. Both impacted with enormous force, making him my hero and antihero, shaping my career ambitions, my understanding of what it meant to be a male, ultimately my view of what a parent and husband should not be like.

Daddy's own father had been intelligent, hardworking, and polite. It gained him a gold watch when he retired (without a pension) from the company where he had worked for fifty years. My father hated his father's boss, he hated the airs of rich kids in school, he had a gut-level identification with the powerless and the poor. And though he had little formal education in politics—not able to afford college—he was a passionately political man. One of my first memories is of coming into the living room in the early morning and seeing him before our large floor radio. He had stayed up all night to find out if Truman would win in 1948.

Despite his lack of college education, Daddy did well in his career. With a natural gift for administration, he became manager of the huge Atlanta Red Cross program in his early thirties. And he used the job in daring ways: desegregating the bathrooms—an unheard of step in the Deep South of the 1950s—hiring the first Jewish doctor to be head of a Red Cross blood program, waging long, victorious battles in defense of such policies against the conservative corporate executives on his board of directors. Then Mother received an inheritance from her father, a successful architect. We moved to the suburbs. Daddy quit his job at Red Cross, planning to "play the stock market" and make real estate investments. More consequentially, he got involved in a new organization, Help Our Public Education (HOPE), which escalated his dissent against southern society.

HOPE formed in response to the threat of "massive resistance" reverberating through the state. The governor and other major Georgia politicians pledged to close all the schools before they would allow blacks into "white education." HOPE's single position was in support of keeping schools open. Daddy was elected president in the spring of 1958, and his name was in the paper.

I woke up in the early morning and heard my parents whispering. Then out the window I saw a wooden cross burning in the yard. The telephone rang, and a voice screamed over the receiver: "We're going to kill all you nigger lovers." The next week over one hundred more calls came, threatening us with bombing, lynching, beatings. The sheriff's house up the street seemed a constant menace—he was rumored to have connections with the Klan.

My father became more and more active in civil rights, working for the Unitarians, then the Quakers, until a band of Nazis tore off his clothes, beat him, and he had a nervous breakdown. In the summer of 1963, after a year's unemployment, he went to work as special assistant to Martin Luther King, and also served on the Executive Board of King's Southern Christian Leadership Conference for four years. Our family moved from Atlanta to Charlotte, Greensboro, and finally back to Atlanta when Daddy started working with King. Most of his brothers and sisters disowned us. One brother, a John Birch Society member in Florida, told his friends we had all been killed in a car crash.

By the time the family returned to Atlanta in the summer of 1963, I was leaving for college at Duke. But my greater interest was civil rights. After years of conflicting emotions and major shifts in my perspective about what I wanted to do, the movement had become my life.

In childhood I expected my someday-career to bear no resemblance to my father's. My plans formed, indeed, partly in rebellion against him and in identification with my mother's frustrated, romantic, and adventurous ideas about what she would have liked to do with her life. For years, my future seemed straightforward and as far from southern society as one could get: I planned to be a space man. From the age of six—when I got a book entitled *Mickey Mouse Goes to the Moon*—until my middle teenage years, space was a passion. I read science fiction, designed rockets, looked through my telescope, wrote stories about trips to other planets. All the stuff of my imagination had to do with such fantasies. I built landscapes that I told other astonished children were worlds from outer space. For Christmas, space costumes, rocket guns, space ships were my standard requests. Flash Gordon Saturday-morning movies formed the highpoint of the week. The army were stellar cadets.

Toward my father directly I felt a confused mix of affection, fear, and suppressed fury. As in Red Cross, Daddy was the administrator of our family's emotional ambiance, ruling as to which feelings were acceptable and real. I watched in guilty admiration my sister's indefatigable revolts against his dictums. I also believed his fables about his sexual, intellectual, and athletic exploits. Underneath, I tried to sort reality from image. Fantasy, space, adventure, reading—all represented escapes into places where the boundaries seemed clearer and the emotional atmosphere more open. As civil rights came to dominate the family's experiences, I also began to realize what it meant to rebel against an entire society.

For several years after the incident with HOPE, I had a kind of double life. Superficially I felt like a "normal teenager." I planned to be an astrophysicist and basked in the glow of post-Sputnik acclaim for my talents in math and science. I had acne. I was absorbed in cross country and track, and alternately terrified and fascinated by girls. But I also lived a vivid subterranean existence, hating myself for being "normal" in ways that bottled up my beliefs about segregation and civil rights.

In 1958 my parents, convinced the public schools would close, sent me to a private school. I had few friends, not much liking the rich kids around me. Finally, I got to know Tyler, a quiet, shy, brilliant boy who shared my aversion to the school's social life and also my budding fascination with ideas in themselves. In the winter, he came over to spend the night. We talked for hours in bed, discussing ping pong, track, our feelings about girls, theology. Then he asked what I thought about integration.

I couldn't speak. It seemed certain to me that if we discussed "the question" our friendship would be over. The silence went on and on, while I pretended to be asleep and raged at myself.

The pattern recurred again and again. Below the surface of school work and girlfriends and track races I felt a growing, vicarious involvement in the civil rights movement, admiration for my father, disgust at my fears. I rebelled against custom in little ways, wearing a flower behind my ear, appearing in an old battered hat. Finally, the pieces of my life began to come together, first with devastating effect, later with great relief.

My girlfriend in Charlotte, where we lived for two years while I was in tenth and eleventh grades, seemed uninterested in my father's civil rights involvement. She was far more concerned about sin and sex—atonement for her sinful thoughts and for our mutual and guilty flirtations around the edges of sinful deeds. Her mother, however, cared considerably more about my father's activities. When freedom riders camped in our yard and FBI agents occasionally followed us on dates—they followed anyone leaving our house—her mother found out. She threatened suicide if we ever saw each other again. The next year we met furtively.

I also began to be more able to speak out. When I went to a Quaker work camp after eleventh grade and met peers who were as liberal as I—and more liberal—I felt exhilarating freedom. That summer we discussed the new movement endlessly. I came home with a new confidence, quit the honorary club that met in a segregated restaurant, withdrew at the end of the year from the state track meet that refused to allow blacks to participate. My hidden feeling toward my parents also came out. That year my father and I spoke mostly through sarcasm and confrontation. But at moments, my parents expressed crucial affirmation. "To my son," Mother wrote a poem shortly after I graduated.

Because our speech so commonly has been
Of school and health, appointments, dress and food,

I realize with sadness and chagrin
Our closest bond perhaps is quietude.
For I have taken refuge in this talk
Fearful lest I too closely might reveal,
Whenever we have shared a pleasant walk,
The sympathy my guarded words conceal.
Know that the thunder of your discontent
Reverberates among my scattered years,
And in the stride of your brave dissent
The outcry of my own youth reappears.
  But where my banner I in prudence furled
  May you unyielding win a better world.

Just as space creatures and alien landscapes had once filled my thoughts, in those years my imagination filled with the shapes, sounds, and feelings of the civil rights movement. In verse more awkward than my mother's, I described what I saw.

   Shadows shuffle
   Across old men, sitting
   Waiting to register while the breeze
   blows rubbish around their feet.

   Old men making gestures on the wall
   Sit and chaw
   Spit, talk quietly

   Creakily an old car and mule pass,
   smelling of dung and hay
   Sullen watchers go by
   red-faced
   narrow-eyed
   waving confederate flags
   stopping to talk to the mayor, in coveralls

   Sweat glistens on the old black faces

   Looking ahead, remembering words:
   "I want my freedom"

The movement was frightening. I remember driving through back streets in small towns of eastern North Carolina where I was helping the Congress of Racial Equality to register blacks to vote. We dashed through alleys, trying to lose the tails of the Ku Klux Klan, then gathered in a small church outside the town, Williamston. All night, men guarded the church against the Klan cars driving by and sometimes firing at us.

After my freshman year at Duke, I went on staff of the Southern Christian Leadership Conference and was sent to St. Augustine, Florida. SCLC had opened the campaign to desegregate facilities in the nation's oldest city on its 400-year anniversary. The press conference called to announce the campaign was covered by the local paper, which also served the neighboring city where my father's Birchite brother was mayor. Daddy was at the press conference with King. When reporters asked why an "outside organization" was coming in, my father replied: "Why, I'm not an outsider at all. My brother is Bill Boyte, over in Lake Wales." The article appeared on the front page.

When I got off the bus and went to the office, dozens of people were badly injured, lying in makeshift beds along the wall. My father, bandaged, was in a corner. The local sheriff, whose brother-in-law was head of the local Klan, had deputized over a hundred Klan members "to keep law and order." They had charged the demonstrators and mercilessly beaten people with nightsticks, chains, and the sharp corners of bricks.

That night I went with Daddy to a motel instead of the SCLC-rented beach cottage where we had originally planned to sleep. When we got out of the car, a shotgun blast shattered the glass. The next day when we went out to the beach, we found the cottage riddled with bullet holes. Klansmen, somehow hearing we had planned to sleep there, had surrounded the building during the night and shot at it from every direction.

Beyond the dangers, however, civil rights was simply inspiring. I found the courage, self-respect, and spirit of the people awesome. Ordinary men and women, janitors and maids and sharecroppers and barbers and dentists, risked their lives, got thrown out of their homes, lost their jobs for the right to register to vote or to sit at a lunch counter. One felt an entire people moving, awakening, the community's buried fabric alive with purpose and vision. I dreamed of a movement that would someday involve, too, people like my grandparents, who had lived their lives with humiliation and shame. In St. Augustine, moreover, I had an experience that made the fantasy seem possible.

Outside the city the police kept demonstrators in what was called the "old jail," a ramshackle brick building. In back, in a crowded, fenced-in square they named the pen, demonstrators would sometimes be forced to stand all day in the hot sun, with no room even to sit. One day my then-current girlfriend, Kathy, who was helping with the movement and had been arrested, got sent to the old jail. I was worried and went after her, to find out how she was.

Kathy was fine, inside the building. We talked for a time through a window. Then I went back to the car. Suddenly six or seven men and a woman converged on me from behind other cars in the lot. They surrounded me. One middle-aged, tattooed man in a large straw hat spoke first. "Well, we've got you now, nigger lover. We know who you are. You're a goddamn Yankee communist."

I was moved to indignant inspiration. "I love blacks and whites," I replied in my most nonviolent vein. Then I added, "but I'm not a Yankee. I grew up in Georgia. And I'm not a communist either. I don't like Russia." "Well, why are you down here, then, causing trouble?" the woman asked.

"What I am is a democratic socialist. I think whites and blacks should get together and fight the fat-assed politicians and big shots who are pushing us all around." The group was silent. Then an older man in coveralls stepped forward and introduced himself. He was the Klan's resident philosopher, of a sort.

"You're a socialist? Hunh. Well, I studied all them philosophies. There's something in that one. But I'm not a socialist. Nor a Christian neither. I'm a Hinduist myself." For several moments we talked about politicians and the rich. Then we shook hands all around and I drove away hurriedly. The next time the Klan had a march through the black section of town, past the SCLC office, my "friend" the Hinduist was in front. I was standing with the crowd of blacks in front of the office. He saw me and waved. I waved back.

I talked about the incident to Andy Young, with whom I was working on voter organization, and with Martin King. It reinforced King's convictions that the movement should begin to address economic as well as social and political questions and that it was time to try organizing poor whites. The next year I experimented with such organizing for SCLC, with little initial success, but the experiences led directly to my later work. The next year also changed my assumptions about myself and my contacts with other people.

Learning to assert and act upon my convictions felt like self-liberation. It also was lonely. The "price" of following my father's example in political activism seemed ineluctably to involve also adopting his kind of male self-definition: toughness, nonchalance and, most of all, independence from emotional attachment. I got contradictory messages from my father—whatever he said, he and Mother were palpably involved in each other's lives and he also was clearly enough eager for other people's respect and affection. But he thought that what he called emotional independence was essential for freedom. A constant refrain from Daddy was "I don't care what anyone thinks." I pretended the same thing.

My involvements in college and with women bore strange similarities. I needed approval from both sources, in different ways. High grades and honors in high school had filled my urge to excel, to be recognized. And college achievement was similarly satisfying. Relations with women, often anxious, met needs to prove my attractiveness, and perhaps even deeper wishes for companionship. But in both instances, I battled my feelings furiously. Why give any credence to the acclaim of an ivory-towered, absurdly pretentious institution like college? I lectured myself constantly. And why be dependent on women when neediness tied me down? I was, after all, a revolutionary, poetic adventurer, a rugged free spirit accountable to no one, destined to be an idealistic soldier of fortune around the world. Feelings of dependency, or affection, were not to be admitted to anyone, or to myself.

My involvements remained truncated. But by the spring of my sophomore year at Duke, it seemed resolved. I was quitting school, planning to work again in the civil rights movement for a short time, and then head out with the Seafarers' Union for unknown adventures. I confidently expected no further serious entanglements in either school work or personal relations.

I had distantly heard Sara's name before we met. She was a junior "campus leader" in the women's college, in a world far removed from the CORE chapter I helped organize. But I didn't connect her name with her presence when I first saw her bicycling down to our demonstration against the Vietnam bombing in February, 1965. My main reaction then was amazement that someone wearing a Duke blazer would join such an event.

We actually met in the morning of the Selma to Montgomery

civil rights march several weeks later, as the crowd swelled to tens of thousands. We spent the day together, holding hands, talking about the movement. When we went back to Duke, we took a walk in the rain for a first date, stopping in a tool shed to describe our life plans. I told Sara I wanted to be a revolutionary traveler. She said she could understand the sentiments but would rather teach. It was my first experience with Sara's sense of herself. She combined a warmth with a sure knowledge of her needs and commitments that I had never seen before.

We married in the summer of 1966. For Sara, our growing involvement had meant postponing and finally foregoing application to graduate school on the west coast. For me, it similarly entailed changes in my life. I decided not to join up with the Seafarers' Union. Then I came back to Duke after a semester's absence.

The summer was a recovery, of parts of myself and my heritage. Tentatively, warily, I began to expose needs and emotions I had long hidden. And in a poor white neighborhood of Durham I gained new pride about my impoverished southern ancestors and found fresh inspiration.

East Durham is the poor-cousin neighbor to the rest of the city, where rows of mill-built houses spread out from the textile plants like spokes of a wheel. The toughest, most impoverished section of East Durham is called Edgemont. Right after we were married, I started organizing among poor whites in Edgemont for the local poverty program, whose efforts previously had been entirely directed to the black community.

Edgemont was in turmoil. Large real-estate interests had begun buying up property, removing white tenants and raising rents, then renting out the houses to blacks who had nowhere else to go (hundreds of black dwellings had been destroyed by a major highway shortly before). Tensions between white and black kids erupted in almost daily fights. White families who had lived in the area for generations were panicking. When I entered the community, the Klan followed in my footsteps, telling people to have nothing to do with "that guy from the nigger outfit." Each house I approached required long moments of hesitation, while I got up the courage to go on the front porch.

Then I met Basie and Doug Hicks. Basie and Doug had lived in East Durham almost all their lives. Their house was the center for the community. They were determined to stay. Basie, a vibrant, militant champion of the neighborhood, was also the source of support for all those in trouble and in need of advice. She was, moreover, eager to extend her warmth to her new black neighbors. "I never agreed with the Kluxers," she would tell others. "Below the skin, blacks have got the same feelings we got, too."

Basie and Doug became leaders of a community group in the area that fought the city power structure on many issues and helped relieve tensions between blacks and whites. Countless stereotype-shattering examples of interracial kindness and goodwill deeply moved me and enabled me to reclaim a southern identity that had often made me feel ashamed.

In the fall of 1967, Sara and I moved to Chicago where I was enrolled in the Chicago Divinity School. Divinity school represented an effort to come to terms with my own childhood religious background, which I had later bitterly rejected, to do theoretical work on the relations between religious themes and political insurgencies, which fascinated me, and to explore the possibilities for an organizing career tied to the church. It was unsuccessful. The distance between my current convictions and the church proved far too wide that year. In Chicago, as a result, my activities were uncertain, and sometimes quixotic. I was involved in antiwar work, in campus activities, and then in the campaign of two radicals running as McCarthy delegates in the Democratic primary. In the campaign my job was to line up organized labor's support for our candidates, against the Daley machine. It took me some time to figure out why union representatives kept forgetting the meetings.

When we reached Chicago, Sara got involved in one of the first women's groups in the country, after finding that the only job she could get—with a master's degree in political science—was as a secretary. Our most intense experiences revolved around women's liberation.

At the time we married, we had made a commitment to have a "democratic relationship." But with no clear models of what that meant, we also tended to fall back on traditional roles. Sara cooked. I washed dishes. Neither of us did much housework, but that which was done seemed "naturally" more nearly Sara's job.

Sara's meeting attendance made me anxious, on a variety of levels. Would she discover secret angers?, I worried. Would women's liberation turn off other men from the movement, or get in the way of the "crucial issues" like the war? Would Sara's widening circle of women friends damage the closeness of our relationship? It was a time of difficult adjustments. But women's liberation also seemed "politically correct." And I was eager for us to re-define our roles in ways that seemed fair. Indeed, it turned out that cooking was much more enjoyable than washing dishes.

We came back to Durham in the summer of 1968. Sara began organizing women's groups. I worked with a community organization project among poor whites, ACT, that a friend had organized during the last year. The project was funded by a large grant from the poverty program, which was eager to build a white constituency. And though they let me come on staff as an assistant director, the agency's administrators felt considerable skepticism about my past civil rights and antiwar activities—a skepticism which, it turned out, was generated by warnings from the local FBI.

My friend, Dick, was a large, handsome man from Connecticut, whose Humphrey Bogart self-image impressed and sometimes intimidated me. It also set the tone for the first stages of the project. Dick had worked with young teenagers and ex-convicts and had hired many staff directly from prison. The hero of the staff had had a shootout with the cops and was a local legend.

The beginning was exciting, romantic—and disastrous. The ex-convicts scared away stable working-class families. I chafed at entering a project whose tone was already so defined, but found myself initially unable to do much to change it. But again Basie and Doug rescued the project. They met with us, told us we were organizing the wrong people. And we listened and changed approaches—under Dick's superficial style were the instincts of a brilliant organizer, which made him immediately understand their warnings. ACT expanded. Through the poor white neighborhood of Durham I saw something of the same exhilarating spirit I remembered from the civil rights movement. For a year, it seemed possible that a new movement was being born, which would have much impact beyond Durham as well.

The excitement of the year made ACT's collapse doubly painful. When the organization demonstrated, got in the papers, and tried to organize people who were not simply poor, the cautious, bureaucratic poverty program clamped down with a vengeance. Political fights, bred by tensions between women and men on staff and between student and community volunteers, flared angrily. In the summer of 1970, the organization ended. Though I continued working with welfare recipients for the next year, my career as a community organizer was clearly closing. Which left my future in a considerable quandary.

For that matter, my institutional career had never been entirely evident. Was I a community organizer? Movement theorizer? Activist? Divinity school and the poverty program job had, in both cases, partly been ways to postpone any final decisions that I didn't know how to make. When ACT fell apart, what institutional context I had was gone. My underlying goal—to help build an interracial movement for justice and democracy—was displaced, at best, to the far distant future.

I briefly turned to writing science fiction, thinking that if I was successful it would free me to do what I wanted in the rest of my time. I wrote a first chapter and outline and sent them off. Then I waited, for months. At last, growing desperate and furious, I wrote the editor at ACE. "I recognize that the frenetic ambiance of New York creates a paralysis of will," the letter went, "but I am, nonetheless, angry at the delay." The editor wrote back, amused. "We have risen above the frenetic ambiance (we thought it was just smog) to find your manuscript and to read it, in the belief that anyone who could swing a mean letter could probably turn out a vibrant ms." Unfortunately, I hadn't. His message was mixed and also illuminating. I was gutsy, assertive—and sabotaging myself. It formed another lesson in my inability to work on projects for purely "mercenary" reasons. But it also left me more uncertain about what I was doing. Moreover, my feelings of uncertainty were compounded by changes in our personal life.

Craig was born in the spring of 1969, in the first year of ACT's success. His infancy created an additional load of fear and responsibility. As Craig grew, I struggled with guilt. My strong, indeed passionate, intention was to be different from my father. Which meant, simply, being available. I felt I should be attentive to nuances of his mood, to his needs, to his every desire for attention. At the same time, guilt made me furious, entrapped, martyred. Finally, one night I picked up Craig and talked to him about my feelings, which we were both beginning to outgrow. He was two and a half, but he understood, and cried, and hugged me.

During this time Sara's work was going progressively better. She loved history. And her dissertation turned out to be an exciting, creative process of self-discovery about her own growing feminism, as well as the consciousness of a generation of young women in civil rights and the new Left. I was proud of Sara's work. And I was competitive at the same time. The job at the poverty program felt like a trap. Our relationship went through a long, painful crisis.

It was, like the first year we met, a turning point, a period of decision and struggle. This time, however, we had more help. Several men from the poverty program and others helped me form a "men's consciousness group," which provided badly needed support for me in uncovering feelings of strength and confidence as I tried to figure out what to do. Sara and I entered a process of marriage counseling, which also aided us immensely in learning to share our fears and needs. And I realized that whatever the risks and ambiguities, I should seek work that I wanted to do and that led toward the longer-range movement I wanted to help build. We made a series of decisions.

When Craig was four and a half, Sara went around the country to interview people for her dissertation. She was gone for many weeks—a separation that scared us all. But we coped well. Craig showed understanding that astonished me. I recorded in my journal some "Craigisms."

To Sara over the phone, in response to her telling him that she loves and misses him: "You should tell Harry that, too."

When I told him I was sorry for being unfair in a fight, and Sara had pointed it out: "Sara has a lot of good ideas. You were being passive aggressive."

When I told him we would have a family council to set rules: "Good, I have a lot of rules I want to say."

When we had a conversation about Johnny, an angry, mixed-up boy Craig knew, I said Johnny was lonely and frightened a lot. Craig said: "I feel that way too, sometimes."

Quitting my job at the poverty program, I had begun writing regularly about political subjects. When necessary, I took odd jobs to support us while Sara finished school.

In one, I was a secretary in a church, and learned what it was like to feel invisible. Once a couple of church deacons came into the office, looking for the minister. He was out. They looked around. Then one turned to the other and said, "We'll have to come back later. No one's here."

In 1975 I went to work in a textile mill as a "hopper feeder." Hoppers are huge machines that look something like monstrous jaws, fed by conveyor belts that stuff raw cotton into a series of metal teeth. The teeth tear up the cotton into small pieces and then deposit the bits on a conveyor belt, which leads to another bank of machines.

I worked the night shift with several other men in what was called the opening room. The temperature rose to well over 100 degrees in the summer nights, and we drank several quarts of water every shift. We also coughed continuously. Dust from the upstairs mingled with cotton fabric to create a thick haze. People who had worked there long had a hard time breathing. The opening room was the worst part of the mill for occupational disease, but other parts were terrible. One night a woman fell off a ledge. The company supervisor ran out and yelled at her for ten minutes, trying to yank her to her feet. He screamed for her to quit malingering and get back to work. Her back was broken. People learned a bitter hatred for the company. I also gained great respect and admiration for the ability of the workers to survive, to comfort each other, and to make decent lives. We talked often about gardens and music.

My jobs furnished a kind of underside to my life. But my real career became political work and writing. I achieved recognition in a Left which struggled to survive during a decade when overt "movement" was all but gone. Our hopes were based far more on faith in the future than on current reality.

In 1971, with other veterans of civil rights, the new Left, the antiwar and women's movements, I helped form a national organization, the New American Movement. Our purpose was grandly proclaimed as building a democratic socialist organization that "would put socialism on the nation's agenda in the 1970s." We planned to break with dogmas that had crippled the Left, speak in a language the American people could understand, articulate a popular and democratic vision of a future society.

Despite the organization's earnest intentions, however, NAM embodied most clearly that sixties-style eschatology that was on a rapid path toward extinction. The goals of transforming American politics, placing socialism on the nation's agenda, recruiting tens of thousands of blue-collar workers, were in sharp dissonance with the sour mood of the Nixon era. The organization survived and even accomplished notable organizing around issues like the Vietnam war and impeachment. But its slow growth and relatively low national profile led many, including many friends, into various forms of disillusionment and an array of colorful fantasies, from the Maharaj Ji to the thoughts of Mao Tse-tung.

For all the problems, however, NAM proved a rare opportunity for me to gain political experience, get published, learn a body of theoretical and historical materials. I wrote, debated, gave speeches, developed programs, built coalitions, traveled around the country. And I learned something about how to fuse my "political side" with my personal feelings, beginning to overcome a sharply etched and old division.

Feminists were active in NAM from the beginning. The organization had a national women's caucus, a regular women's bulletin, and several "women's chapters" like the Charlotte Perkins Gilman chapter organized by Sara and others in North Carolina. NAM sponsored a national conference on socialism and feminism in the fall of 1972, and initiated another, much larger meeting several years later. At least half of NAM's national leadership and staff were to be filled with women. And NAM consequently furnished a fascinating and important opportunity for men and women alike to experiment with new roles.

Men's reactions were often defensive, guilty and sullen. As one man described his experiences: "After a while you learn new patterns of avoidance and submissiveness." Yet other reactions surfaced. Men's caucuses appeared at conventions and national meetings. Men sought to learn how to support each other more openly, and to express anger in ways that were constructive and honest. Men also learned how to be more "open" and vulnerable. It was a welcome lesson.

In 1972 I published, with a friend, a long piece that criticized the traditional "Leninist model" of Left political organization, arguing that it was not appropriate for the complex, qualitative discontents and the political environment of advanced industrial society. The paper created a storm of controversy on the Left, was reprinted, attacked, discussed in many forums. It also helped define NAM's political identity more clearly. And it made Frank and me quickly well known in the Left environment.

I enjoyed the recognition, and it scared me as well. Indeed, the new dilemma brought to the surface old fears. My feelings and needs for companionship were much more vivid than ever before in my life. And at the same time, success seemed to threaten a kind of impersonality—I dreaded the thought that people would see me only as a "Left celebrity," and never as a person like them. At the end of a national meeting I finally spoke about my fears. Afterwards I cried among friends, and received a great outpouring of warmth and support.

In the mid-seventies our family's life changed again. By that time I was writing more and more regularly, and embarked on a series of political questions—about corporate politics, grass roots organizing, Left strategy—that were to provide material for years of work. Politics too was on a modest upswing. I pushed hard for unity among different Left groups, became active in the Democratic Socialist Organizing Committee, a group started by Michael Harrington and others, as well as NAM. And new, exciting signs of movement and activism became visible in North Carolina. Sara's graduate school was ending with indications that her dissertation would become a fine, successful book.

In 1976 my father got lung cancer. It was excruciatingly difficult to talk about his dying, about my sadness and loneliness. But I also felt we had reached a new kind of reconciliation, with mutual respect and acceptance. Shortly before he died, I taped his memories about Red Cross and civil rights, a legacy for the future.

In the same year we had to make a decision about moving either to New York or Minneapolis, both cities in which Sara had job offers. The process of choosing again tested our relationship. My first impulse was to insist on moving to the east coast, where political work and publishing opportunities seemed, on the surface, much greater. But we decided, finally, to come to Minnesota, partly on the advice of an old friend who disabused us of any illusions about New York, partly because Sara's job in Minnesota was more secure and open-ended. My difficulties with finding a secure career in political work and writing were not to be completely resolved for the next several years. They remained anxious, uncertain, often nerve-racking as life choices. But the move turned out well, an adventure nonetheless, and a beginning.

3
Humping It
Over the Hump
(or)

*I Keep Shoveling on the Off-chance That
There Is a Pony Around Here Somewhere*

by Paul B. Fiddleman

PROLOGUE

How do you start something like this without setting off on an
ego trip?

In attempting to put this together I thought of a TA (Transac-
tional Analysis) trick for identity-definition. What would I like to
be written on a T-shirt that I was wearing so that everyone could

see it? (The kicker is then to write what should appear on the back so that people could see what you really are affirming, once you have passed by.) Mine reads in front: "Yea, though I walk through the valley of the shadow of death I shall fear no evil, 'cause I'm the meanest sonofabitch in the valley." And in back: "Don't always believe everything you read." In re-reading these lines I would like to add an amendment to the back message: "Don't shit upstream if you live downstream."

I Identify Myself, Partially

I share many of the attributes, statistically, of Mittelmensch American. I am forty-four. (I think I am forty-four. I have noticed that in the past few years my age does not come to me as quickly as it did twenty or even thirty years ago. I figure that when you are younger, and only partially enfranchised, your age is important, not to mark one's span of time on earth, but as an anchor point to mark off the distance between lack of status and becoming officially sanctioned as reaching same. At the moment, my age provides me little intrinsic reward. It is no longer a matter of being old enough to get a driver's license, or to quit school, or to join the army, or to legally drink in a bar. I have gone beyond those legal milestones and can now, without fear of exposure: drive a car; stay out late; make it with my lady [more accurately, my wife] without worrying about outraged parents, the threat of pregnancy, getting caught . . . ; get a loan without too much hassle; obtain somewhat respectful attention from public servants, bank tellers, shopkeepers, etc.; in short, I am totally and legally emanicpated.) As can be recognized immediately, I have some difficulty keeping to the point.

I am also married to the same woman I began with (which does make me somewhat of a recent statistical deviant), have two children, two cars, one house—owned but not entirely paid for—live in the suburbs of a small southern university town, and make somewhat above the median middle-class income. I am a psychologist. More specifically, I am a clinical psychologist, well credentialized with necessary Ph.D., legitimized with state license, less well credentialized with a modest number of publications, but provided some degree of job security by being a tenured faculty member of a well-regarded and nationally recognized state university.

In re-reading the last few paragraphs, I am struck with something that was not initially apparent to me. Although I mention my profession last, I actually spend a great deal of time discussing it, or, more to the point, editorializing about it. This immediately suggests to me, as a legitimized expert in human motivation, that although I imply that my occupation has somewhat low valence or importance, in fact, it is considerably more important to me than I am willing to admit. Aha! Could this smack of ambivalence? Yes, it could.

In fact it does. After almost eighteen years of professional activity, as well as six years of graduate training and the obligatory four years of undergraduate preparation, I still have not gotten it totally clear in my head as to just where I do stand in regard to my profession. I am still ambivalent about my occupation, a recognition that does not bother me nearly as much as I somehow think it should. It's not an ambivalence based on a questioning of competence or value, but more a mind-set that if something else came along which seemed either more lucrative or more enjoyable, I would not have too many major doubts about drastically changing my profession. The doubts I would have would be more related to an unwillingness to give up what has become a very comfortable and familiar life style, one that does not require too much expenditure of energy (or, at times, thought) and that clearly provides my family and me a very secure base from which to move around. I honestly don't think that I have any burning desire to somehow prove myself, or to make more of a mark than I have; it's just that I find that much of my professional investment is involved in doing a good job, not as a means of somehow advertising or justifying my worth.

The ambivalence (or to be totally accurate, a less than complete commitment to my profession) tends to manifest itself in a number of ways. It results in an almost complete isolation of my job from the rest of my life. While mine is not a traditional forty-hour week, I do find that for the most part, when I leave work, the work leaves me. When I do carry materials home, it is because I have a deadline to meet, and even then, more often than not, I bring the materials back to work the following day to complete. My after-hours recreation and reading interests have very little to do with my occupation. When I am on vacation, other than those rare times when I can combine some business with pleasure in the form of a travel grant,

I manage to avoid both references to and thoughts about professional matters. Even when I browse through the book stacks at the university library, I never approach shelves containing books on psychiatry or psychology. Further, when I do have evening work, I make a special point to complete it at home and not in my departmental office.

I am both amazed and somewhat mystified by the number of colleagues who spend their evenings in their offices or laboratories. My question often is whether my colleagues are not getting much gratification at home, or whether I am missing something basic at work. Particularly in the areas involving services to people, like medicine and the ministry, it seems that much too often one's work demands are used as a barrier to avoid family obligations. One does his homework everywhere but home. I can see why this happens. One can get so many more positive strokes from grateful others than from one's family, which tends to see this larger-than-life personage in a frequently less than flattering light. It's much easier to get this positive regard when you don't have to follow through, and just do your good deed and split. It's easy to do and very seductive, but it plays hell with any adequate family life. I've mused at times about what would happen if we declared certain professions as dangerous or injurious to continued family life, sort of a Surgeon General's warning.

Getting back to my point. I have deliberately separated my family life from my work life, even to the extent that my wife and I have very little contact with colleagues other than those happily rare, semiobligatory university or hospital functions. Our attendance is at best only so that we are not considered wholly antisocial. Frankly, shop talk, other than in the shop, bores the hell out of me.

Besides my own ambivalence, though, there is an ambivalence built into the profession itself. Clinical psychology is the only one of the helping professions that still maintains its base in academia. Medicine, nursing, social work, have all evolved to special training, in separate schools, with their own deans, guidelines, and requirements. Clinical psychology, on the other hand, is closely tied to the strictly academic, liberal arts tradition in which direct practical use of your training is considered, if not out-and-out prostitution, at least presumptive evidence that one is doing some active amateur or semipro hooking.

I discuss this somewhat unusual situation because my role is even more unusual and contributes in part to my ambivalence. I am actually neither academician nor clinician, but both at once. I am a full-time, academically legitimized, tenured faculty member, who keeps equally validly acquired offices in both the university and the state hospital. For some reason this confuses most administrators and I have found it easier to indicate that I am rented, or perhaps more accurately, indentured to the hospital. While my salary is provided through the university on university checks, the money is obtained through the business office of the hospital. As a result, I am claimed by both institutions but actually belong to neither, and therefore cannot be comfortably fitted into either organization's administrative chain of command. I can't be fired because no one quite knows to whom I belong. While this clearly has marked advantages in terms of escaping from institutional pressure or surveillance, it can play havoc with your identity.

Other than this split identity, I find it a rather positive condition. I can be either one or the other, or neither, depending on whim, policy, or which affiliation represents an immediately viable sanctuary. Moreover, I am able to be critical of both institutions since my partial affiliation provides a chance for a bit more objectivity than those people can have who are more deeply mired. The danger is either dilettantism or cynicism, and in more honest moments I have to plead guilty on both counts.

I have found that my academic role provides me less gratification than my clinical role. Part of the reason is status. In the clinical-hospital setting my academic credentials enhance my status, whereas in the university community my off-campus work is viewed as a sign of second-class citizenship. A more important reason is values, mine versus the university's. I see in the academic world an increasingly narrow focus on ideas as ends-in-themselves, with more concern for research production than for the uses and consequences of those ideas. I knew someone in a zoology department, for example, who was concentrating his research on a parasite that lived within a liver fluke that survived within the liver of a local frog. He had managed to reduce his world to the "ultimate worm." This issue has more than abstract interest to me. In the Army, working in a research and development laboratory, I saw a sequence of technical breakthroughs, each of which individually was an impressive achievement but all of which, hooked up together, formed an incredibly lethal weapon system. When working with planaria flatworms in one laboratory emerges as a weapon placed in a very effective delivery system at the other end, and with none of the producers at the various junctures feeling either concern or guilt, then we are in trouble.

What really scares me is how easily we can encapsulate our ideas and even our work so that we deliberately deny ourselves a glimpse of the "big picture." We become so turned on to the praise, self or other, which follows our expertise, that we avoid looking down to the end of the assembly line. In that way we comfortably commit technological atrocities—like the member of a firing squad who becomes so proud of his marksmanship that he forgets what he just put a jagged hole into. Reading about the Nazi extermination process, I am struck by the fact that almost every major figure who was involved denied being involved in the end product. One man made sure that the communities were evacuated, another kept the train scheduled on time, a third made certain selections, while a fourth transported hydrocyanic acid to a receptacle. No one really killed anyone. As one historian has noted after reading these depositions, it was his distinct impression that the victims managed to kill themselves and then disposed of their own cadavers. While systems, political as well as scientific, provide a legitimizing sanction to this diffusing of responsibility, I am dismayed to recognize how so many of us are capable of avoiding culpability by narrowing our field of vision. Referring back to the Prologue, I do live downstream. So do all of us.

I Identify Myself a Bit More Completely

All right. I have expounded at length about what I am not, or why I am not what I should be. Now then, what am I? Basically, I am a practitioner of an art or a skill that looks deceptively simple from the outside. At least, a great many people with no training fancy themselves as being capable of practicing it.

My skills, training, and experience allow me to do what I do, and I do it well. I was not born a psychologist, nor did I develop certain attributes in my childhood or during my first twenty-one years which made me a "natural." My profession is not one that you are genetically predisposed to, or as the standard folklore has it, that you choose because the alternative choice is patienthood. This is nonsense. I've been around enough to see that there are as many maniacs, freaks, whackos, and garden-variety nuts in psychology as in any other profession.

Well then, if I was not born to the profession, or so directed because of early recognition of special attributes, or because I was barely one step ahead of the men with the nets, then why and how do I find myself, in my middle years, a psychologist, and a semiacademic one at that? I honestly believe that I reached here through a number of choice-point decisions, some motivated by logical and rational thought, but most of them resulting from random choices arrived at with about as much care as flipping a coin. In retrospect, I see no grand plan, no purposeful goal-directing, no driving ambition, no role model whom I wished to emulate, no working through problems or traumas, and no financial or status considerations. What I do see is a whole series of crossroads where choices had to be made and where each choice eventually confronted me with another set of possible choices. While some choice-point decisions were carefully thought out, some were made impulsively, and others I just sort of drifted into.

Like most people I know, I went through adolescence without much direction, without much investment other than in some immediate and usually physical gratification. What tends not to be remembered by those of us who lived through the 1950s is that it was not only a time of noninvolvement, but also a time when no one really bothered you unless you wanted to be bothered or you bothered other people. Even the prototypical hyper-vigilant mothers, with whom we all seemed to be saddled, really tended to stay off our respective cases as long as we (a) came home with most of our appendages and other crucial body parts intact; (b) remained in school, even if barely so; and (c) did not knock up the dirty little girl around the block and have to marry her, thus being forced to drop out of school, get a low-paying job and raise our children in a different faith (if not race). Other than these injunctions, nobody bothered you. As long as you stayed at least psychologically close to home, you could avidly and ferociously flog your winkie for hours until the damn thing fell off in your hand. Underachievement was met with a despairing shake of the head, a sigh that either shattered or rattled windows for miles around, an obligatory glance upward, and, if really pushed, The Mother's Curse. No one was sent to the shrink or the child-guidance center. That was reserved for the really first-class, wholly dedicated lunatic.

I went to college because I was supposed to go to college. I never asked why—it was expected, my father graduated from college, I was expected to follow. For someone who makes his living by asking "why?" I am shocked to think back and realize that I never asked why about much of anything.

These last few paragraphs have helped clarify something that has bothered me for years. Ever since my own children were born I have been surprised by a vague need to visit home every year or so, particularly now as the kids have been growing into their own identities. Yet, each time I would visit I would return with an equally vague feeling that I hadn't done what I set out to do. Something was missing. While writing these paragraphs, I understood this vagueness. I had been looking for the thread that hangs all this together, the "why," the game plan. Now I realize there never was any, that I have been trying to superimpose some kind of artificial order or sequence when none ever existed. I have just returned from a week-long visit, and for the first time in years there is no sense of incompleteness.

As a teenager I also did not get very far in asking "why not?" which, in this case, meant dropping out of college. In the early fifties, one did not drop out of college if one had the ability; one flunked out, or didn't go at all. One's direction, it seems, is shaped by the availability of external supports—a paved road as opposed to a dirt one. And shaped also by the barriers flanking the road. My one-month search for jobs following a less than monumental first-semester freshman year brought home the fact that I was unskilled, except for carrying golf bags—a difficult occupation to maintain in midwinter New York City. One other alternative was the military, and although it surely represented an escape hatch if all else failed, there were some definite realities to be considered, including a still-fulminating Korean police action. Further, having just declared partial independence from a militantly over-protective mother, and actually succeeding, I didn't want to push my luck too hard with her. Prevailed upon by parents, and grudgingly admitting that I offered damn little to a sluggish job market, I allowed myself to be convinced of the value of continuing an education, and returned to school.

Now comes the moment which I have been vaguely dreading. At the risk of oversimplifying, my crucial occupational choices began when I wouldn't study American history. Now, that reads as stupid as it sounds, and has always sounded to me. I hold, however, that my refusal to take American history courses in college is the single most significant choice I made in my career. It was probably the first real choice I ever made.

According to a note I received from some dean during the middle of my sophomore year, it was time to declare a major course of study. With as little goal-directedness as usual, I checked out my courses and decided that since I had done best in history, that would be my major, and besides I kind of liked history. So, I became a history major. With what, in retrospect, must have been either incredible naïveté or late blooming of adolescent omnipotence, I also formulated the position that, since I was a history major, I ought to be able to take the kind of history courses I wanted. Sure, easy, just like the rest of my already distinguished scholastic career. An adviser informed me otherwise. Refusing to take any courses in American history meant that I could not be a history major, since American history was required—no, demanded—by the History Department. But I had made up my mind; no American history for me. So I had to seek out another major and I chose psychology, having already taken six hours of courses and done fairly well. By such mundane motivations are great careers launched.

It seems that much of my career has been based on such decisions made at critical choice points, though with less negativism and somewhat more rationality. The choice of a graduate school, once I realized that such was necessary, became easier when I was rejected by all but one school. My original choice was not based on a particular program or nationally known figure, but rather on what I thought would be a good locale to attend school.

A choice with much more direct significance for my current professional activity confronted me when I was completing the doctorate. I had two alternatives; one was to stay at the university supported by a National Science Foundation postdoctoral fellowship and then join the faculty of the medical school as a researcher, the other was to accept a three-year interdisciplinary postdoctoral fellowship in neurology and neurophysiology at one of the northeastern medical schools. This second option would have allowed me not only to follow my research interests, but also to accrue two years of medical school during the three years. And it would have opened a number of other options. What do you do with a Ph.D.-M.D.? Do you practice or do you begin to carve out a research career? As dilemmas go, this ain't a bad one to be involved in.

Unfortunately, these kinds of equally positive options make me obsess, and I don't fare very well as an obsessive. Obsessing triggers a part of my collective unconscious wherein a long-gone Talmudist, capable of arguing both sides of an issue with equal plausibility, becomes activated. I find that while arguing one point I am busy collecting support for the opposite position. I finally resolved the dilemma by deciding that the northeast was not really a good place to live and accepting the NSF fellowship.

But a more fundamental problem remained unsolved. Even at that point I had begun to entertain some doubts about my profession and where I was heading in it. These doubts, if anything, increased during the year, and what began as a prestigious fellowship followed by what looked like a successful research career, became more and more of a burden. It's very difficult for me to put my finger on the etiology. Certainly there were sufficient external as well as internal rewards. My community was a gathering place for interesting people, especially a large group of unattached women in their mid-twenties; to describe it as a high-class meat market would be quite accurate. In addition, given the fellowship and a small but solid reputation in research at the medical school, I had an abundance of job security. But I also had a growing sense of wrongness about the whole situation. On the one hand, I felt that I had to get out and get some distance, but on the other hand I found it easier to do nothing and sail with what had become a comfortable trade wind.

I have never been sure whether this ambivalence reflected my doubts about my professional worth or whether it realistically appraised my less-than-complete commitment to a research career. Whatever it was, it was one hell of a time to develop second thoughts about a career. Even fifteen years later I can still conjure up some of the gut wrench and discomfort. The more I talked to others in the labs, the more I discovered that my dilemma wasn't at all unusual. According to the consensus, if I just held out and didn't go off half-cocked, it would all resolve itself. But I kept worrying; what if it didn't resolve itself? And meanwhile I would be going deeper into my work, making it more difficult for me to get out. Again the obsessive rumination and Talmudic balancing of evidence on both sides, more and more intense as the end of the fellowship period approached and would force me to make a decision. What I did was quit, on the last day of the fellowship, and packed and got out of town as fast as I could, about as scared as I have ever been. I had at best only a vague idea of where I was going and even less formulated plans about what I was going to do once I got there.

I still think that I made a good decision. I've seen too many men my age who continue to have doubts about their choice of profession. These doubts never really get resolved, but the investment in their occupation becomes such that a drastic change will expose them and their families to some economic and social risk. I like to think that the risk would be worth it. Of course, it's easy for me to say that when I have little reason for making such a significant change. I have to be honest and state that, considering the responsibilities I now have, I doubt that I would quit as I did seventeen years ago. I would like to think that I would do it if I had as many doubts as I did then, but I am also rather glad I don't have to check that out.

I spent three months working around the country at a variety of odd jobs including pumping gas, delivering groceries, being a short-order cook, and other occupations invovling no training and little requirement for longevity. I tended to work for a week or two, make enough money to be able to move on, then drive up the road a few hundred miles and find an interesting place and stop again. There was no plan, nor any real purpose or direction. I needed to find out something about myself.

Finally, after accumulating a few hundred dollars, I did what I had always wanted to do: become a dealer in Las Vegas. This had been one of my prevailing fantasy outlets, the kind of thing you kick around at 1:30 in the morning before a final paper or an important exam, when you wonder why you are putting yourself through all this crap. I figured, what the hell, let's try it. So I did. I managed to get a job as a shill at a local casino on Fremont Street, playing the empty tables to bring in shy customers with a ten-dollar house chip and my shy, guileless, open, boyish face. I also enrolled in a dealer school, run by an old pro, and began to learn the trade. After six weeks I learned that I didn't like it all that much and quit. I moved to California and crashed with a friend while I looked around for a job.

It was at this time that I began to realize something. Quietly, but very definitely, I was beginning to detach myself from my center. I was losing it. Even if I was trying my hardest to enjoy downward mobility, for better or worse I had grown up middle class. I had values, expectations, a script, and certain interpersonal skills which had worked. When you break away from these, it's going to take some time to find alternatives. I was finding them but I wasn't all that comfortable with what I found. A lot of moving around, a lot of alcohol and some soft drugs, a bunch of different sights and smells, and I began to feel unhappy, even scared.

I also realized that I wasn't all that competent with my new options. Case in point: when challenged in a crummy bar in Barstow, California, because you have picked up a local girl who is vaguely the property of someone else, do you (a) haul your ass out, figuring that it's his turf; (b) try to bluff your way out of it; (c) hit him with anything you can reach; or (d) do something else. Now this is something that most people who spend great gobs of time in crummy bars know how to handle. I didn't. Along with recognizing my incompetence, I also came to the very discomfiting realization that while I had one foot in a bar, I had the other ready to move back, *if* I wanted to. I would never wholly deal with my new options because I always knew that if things got too nasty, I could get back to my nice academic-professional environment. The people around me were stuck where they were and had to make the best of it. I had become a dilettante blue-collar worker, and a kind of half-assed one at that. What now? I did what everyone did when faced with an identity crisis; I sorted it all out by joining the Army.

The next three years can be boiled down to a single lesson; if you are responsible for one step in a sequence of events which results in an immoral or destructive outcome, then you are as responsible as the person who pushes the final button. I learned this lesson while participating in a variety of classified research-and-development projects, many of them calling upon university scholars' expertise. It became very easy, I discovered, to work diligently on a project without having to be reminded or even to become aware of the implications of the information you were providing. An anthropological evaluation of a Vietnam subcultural group, for example, would—when translated into an Army Area Study—produce massive disturbances in that subculture. My first-hand witness of the consequences that these reports levied upon people's lives had a profound effect. Ever since, I have felt an almost fanatical concern with consequences of our actions.

There was a big difference, as it turned out, between feeling and doing. When I was about to be released from the Army, I applied to a variety of research and development civilian think-tank programs. My thinking was that, given a four-year distancing from psychology, my most realistic approach was to work in the areas with which I had the most familiarity—namely, limited warfare. That is how I acted, despite my increasingly strong personal indignation about where such research was leading us. Here was my first exposure to how material needs make ugly dents in our moral façade.

I also encountered, for the first time, the "thin letter syndrome." Thirty out, thirty back, no job, impressive credentials, valuable experience, but. . . . Given my prior crossroad decisions, all involving my choice, I found that choices you make are very closely contingent on choices you have. The choices I eventually had were between a research job in the midwest and a call from my major professor who asked me if I wanted to come back to my southern university. Again, major decisions were made on less than totally rational grounds. ("The midwest—Jesus Christ—it's flat and hot, and they have tornadoes and big bugs, and the people talk kind of peculiar.") I also came back because I needed some resolution of my still active ambivalence.

I Identify Myself in Other Ways

My military experience provided me with something else than moral lessons. I acquired along the way a wife and a child. Again I am struck with the randomness of so much that happens to us. If I hadn't joined the Army, and hadn't requested an assignment which was as far as possible from direct psychological services, I would never have met my wife and, along those same lines, would never have had my first child. But other sorts of chance were even more influential. Spouses are often acquired, I believe, by choice, which is almost entirely a function of who is around when you decide to choose and of what your needs seem to be at that point in your life.

So I married her. Getting married is easy, at least the technical sequence. You need a woman (or man), a certain amount of money for a license, a certain minimum of age, and a negative Wassermann test. With all four, anyone can do it. Then it gets difficult.

What became very clear, within a month or so of our marriage, was that we were going to have to work like hell to make it work. My wife and I are very different in almost all respects—attitudes, values, background, experience, and virtually everything else you might think of. According to the usual criteria of marital experts, our marriage probably will fail. Yet we have made it work and work well. We have bargained, negotiated, made deals, compromised our values, gotten pissed at each other, traded off, switched roles and then switched back again and, wonder of wonders, we are still married. Individually and together we are very different people than we were when we began. Speaking honestly, I'm not sure that I am a better person for these changes. I am, however, a much better husband.

The success of our marriage has derived most of all, I think, from our ability to shift and change roles. But that ability developed only after some painful time had passed. My initial expectation of how to be a husband, and my expectation of how my wife should be a wife, were based on my perception of my parents' marriage. I grew up in a family where the prevailing attitude of the women was that men were basically not all that bright or competent. Without the direct and assertive guidance by his reality-oriented wife, they believed, a husband would wander off and get either lost or run over. My father, on the other hand, was from that kind of traditional family where one's wife was required, literally, to follow her husband, in a respectful posture, two or three paces behind. Only after attending to his needs and the needs of the children could she get around to doing anything about hers.

Because of these extreme positions, the one-down partner in "the marriage" became a skillful guerrilla fighter. There was no payoff in directly confronting the powerful partner; that simply got him or her banged around, physically as well as psychologically. The option then was to try to undercut the other partner, to sabotage, to get a point across by sniping from the trees or setting up emotional boobytraps. It cost them too. My parents eventually divorced, not only because they ran out of the convenient fiction about keeping it together for the children, but also because tearing large gaping holes in each other's viscera lost some of the enjoyment, or maybe it just hurt too much. An interesting case for psychomatic medicine: within six months after their separation, both had experienced major organ malfunction, which remains to this day.

What I derived from these examples was a profound sense of the almost total waste of ability and effectiveness as a human being that such a low-key, but intensely painful, marriage produced. Both my parents are really good people, but they severely truncated what growth potential they had. My model from both of them was simply this: it's got to be better than that.

My wife came from a family where the men called most of the shots, decided what was happening and when, and made all the major, as well most of the minor, decisions for the family. Women were not tied exclusively to *kirche, kuche,* and *kinder,* but they had better be proficient in those as well. They were allowed to grow and expand, but only within limits and only after asking permission.

Question: What happens when the son of two skilled guerrilla warriors meets the daughter of a benevolent despot? In the proper scenario, each should haul ass back to where it is safe and familiar— my wife to dating West Point and Annapolis underclassmen; myself to the competitive and hard-nosed ladies who were so much fun to challenge.

My wife and I started our marriage with these role models. We soon realized, however, that they produced "victories" that were painfully hollow and, in the long run, emotionally expensive for us and our kids. So we began to set up negotiations and began to make deals with each other. A small example: In order to give her a few hours alone at least one evening a week, I took the kids with me while doing the weekly grocery shopping. Ten years later, grocery shopping has become almost entirely my responsibility. We also began to share jobs, training each other and then trading off when we needed to. There is no reason that I cannot take care of our two children and the house, while my wife goes on a week's vacation with her parents, any more than she is able to do so when I am gone. I may not be able to cook and clean and keep things running as efficiently as she can and does, but neither do things fall apart. On the other hand, she can and does balance the checkbook and handle the general finances, including taxes, better than I do. In short, we have taken a whole series of traditionally sex-linked roles and responsibilities and unlinked them.

When we began to get the hang of this switching off, my wife decided that she wanted to go back to school and finish her degree. We worked out a schedule and she started the process, first at night school to make up some nontransferable credits, then three years later in a full-time degree program. Nursing school is a particularly stressful type of training, what with the long hours, with heavy academic as well as emotional demands, and with a philosophy that being pushed to the limit makes you a better nurse and builds character. In fact it does neither. What it did for us, however, was to allow us to begin making a number of changes in our relationship.

I might have easily resented her decision to take on these new demands when she was not wholly fulfilling her demands at home. In fact, her decision pleased me because I had begun to see in her the stagnation that often afflicts mothers in their early thirties. She had withdrawn so far from any investment in the outside world that she had become almost wholly dependent on me for stimulation and support. Her long years of study were difficult, at times painful and frustrating, but worth it to us. We looked upon the nursing program as an adventure, something to be overcome and defeated. When she finished, in a lot of ways both of us felt that *we* had earned a BSN degree.

I am extremely proud of her and tend to brag about her whenever I can. Despite being twelve to fifteen years older than her classmates, she graduated with honors, was chosen by the national honors society for nurses, and then took on what is probably the most difficult kind of nursing—pediatric intensive care. All of this has enhanced her confidence and sense of autonomy. It has also enhanced my own. I no longer feel obligated to "entertain" or stimulate her with news of the outside world, and I no longer have to consider time spent away from home as somehow taking from her the only stimulation she has in life. On the contrary, because we are into such different kinds of work, we provide added enrichment for each other.

I am not sure of the impact of my wife's work on our children. They are both very independent, capable kids, with firm ideas about the way they want things to be. We may not agree with them, or support them in their goals, but we do manage to give them a fair hearing. I think they are our points of vulnerability. We can get hurt through them, and often we worry too much about how happy they are at the moment, which means that their hurt becomes our hurt, something that makes us even more vulnerable.

If there is any sort of a "plan" which we have decided on in raising the children, it is to reduce, as much as possible, their feeling of obligation toward us. We have both seen how a strong sense of obligation to parents easily becomes a painful and destructive guilt trip. I don't think children owe their parents very much. What we give them is not in exchange for love and respect, but something we feel we should do or wish to do for them.

I think my ability to give them examples, both positive and negative, of how I am and, moreover, to give them a clear statement of my attitudes and my positions on issues, has been important in raising them. I don't expect them to slavishly and almost reflexively follow my values, nor even to overtly agree with them. All I want is that they see me clearly, prejudices, blind spots, illogicality, and all. My kids have seen my feet of clay, in fact they have seen my clay feet clear up to my ass. I don't ask their forgiveness; it isn't theirs to give, or mine to accept. But I hope I can count on their tolerance.

I have noticed that my children manage to remember as well as repeat, with at times unnerving accuracy, certain low spots in my behavior. Our so-called "Mrs. Lloyd Story"—regarding an unfortunate loss of my coordination as well as judgment following overindulgence at a very fine English lady's home after she invited us visiting Americans to share her hospitality—still sends them (and, I darkly suspect, their friends) into paroxysms of laughter. Yet, while embarrassing, there seems to be a lot of real affection involved even in their relating of something I wish were left in London.

I totally love my kids, but I am fond of them as friends as well. We can go off and wander through shopping malls, or play ball, or argue, or just sit around being useless, without any need for lecture, direction, or example. It's easy raising them, and I just hope it is as easy being raised.

On Reaching a Milestone
and Looking Back

Having safely gotten over the forty hump without utter disaster, I can look back and, with as much objectivity as I am capable of, begin to add up some pluses and minuses. Like any survivor and veteran, I have bragging rights and give myself permission to tell war stories.

I realize and accept (not without some sadness) that my fantasies at eighteen or twenty-one have not in any way been gratified. I think that much of the fortieth-year depressions, or the sudden and compulsive need to modify one's life, involves just that—the realization that our fantasies have died. We seem all to have formulated some goals which we would reach before we finished growing up. For some of us these were vague, for others very specific and concrete. As far as I was concerned, at eighteen as well as twenty-one, I wanted only two things: to make a million dollars and to lay Brigitte Bardot. Not very impossible dreams, only improbable outcomes. Did I reach them? I didn't even get within sniffing distance of either. But you know, it doesn't matter, not at all.

What does matter now? What is the feeling that survives inside this veteran? It's the sobering realization that not only am I no longer traveling uphill, but that I have reached the top and have now started downhill with increasing velocity. That even if I were to encounter BB, I'm not sure I could do her justice. Moreover, she's almost as old as I am!

It seems more than that, though. It's realizing that I am two steps slower and that if I am thinking of making any significant life-style changes, they are going to be more difficult. And besides, I have others dependent on me. I can see why I am getting a bit more conservative. Partly it's the fear that if I deviate too far from where I am, I might get lost, and might not ever find myself again. It also involves jealousy of those who either have not yet made it or who just have and who are beginning to get the payoffs that I now enjoy. It's like holding close to yourself the one thing you can do better than anyone else you know, and hoping no one learns to do it better. And it's having the kind of special courage to be able to yell, "Hey, I'm still here, I'm still hanging in there swinging, and maybe I can't hit it as far as I used to, but I know what's coming, and because of that I may be able to slice one to the opposite field and catch someone napping."

That brings me to something else that we owe others as well as ourselves. If we are lucky, and are good at our craft, maybe we can teach someone else. The problem is that all our apprentices move out and seek their own apprentices. I guess what counts is to be able, gracefully and with good humor, to accept the fact that in reaching for autonomy, they must deny their dependence on their mentors. And to recognize that what really counts is not receiving obligation from apprentices, but seeing that they do a job well, maybe even better than we could have done it.

What has helped me is my willingness to move into other areas of my profession. I may act cynical about my job, but it does allow me a certain degree of flexibility and independence. I have tried to get into consulting in new areas whenever I can. Most of the time I do this gratis. In my profession at least, expertise never changes, and what I can bring to a program is expertise. And so in the past ten years I have developed consulting relationships in areas as diverse as prisons, both state and federal, community mental health clinics, state hospitals, orphanages, drug programs, rape and women's assault centers, alcoholism programs, and others. I earn not only a feeling of accomplishment, but also some gratification that I haven't received at the university, and maybe that's what the payoff really is.

I can also say that I have done a fairly good job sharing the raising of my kids. When I see them respecting others, and not hurting people deliberately, even if they deserve it, and protecting those who can't protect themselves, then I think, "not bad, not bad at all."

And when I look at my wife, and see how much she has grown, not because I grew her, but because I gave her the room to grow without demanding my rights or dues, and when I see the pride she takes in herself, then I realize that all we did together to make that happen has been well worth it.

When I read this over, it sounds like an obituary, and I didn't mean to have it come out that way. There's more coming, a lot of crossroads and choice points.

Could I have done things differently? Hell yes, everything. Would it have been better if I had? Who knows? I tried tracing back a few alternative choice-point possibilities, but I got confused, since I don't know what would have happened had I taken that turn. I know that a lot of people believe in some celestial game plan. I don't. If I learned nothing else from my time in Las Vegas, it was that if you play long enough, the house always wins.

I don't think I'm going to get very far in changing me, and in looking back, I think I haven't really ever changed very much. I don't play the game better now, but I have become a more gracious winner and a somewhat less surly loser because I think I understand the rules a little bit better.

4
Gestures Toward the First Person

by Peter Filene

One morning in June of 1969, I took off my wrist watch and put it on a shelf. During the next week I must have glanced at my bare left wrist a dozen times a day, then less often, finally not at all. When I saw my watch curled on the shelf, silent and dusty and permanently 8:33, I smiled in triumph. Goddamn, I was free! Without that little silver machine, I could not calculate how much time I was "spending," how much I was "wasting," how far "behind" or "ahead" I was moving, all those calculations of achievement and guilt, work and nonwork, that I had learned to make in twenty-nine years.

We had come for the summer from Chapel Hill, North Carolina, to Cambridge, Massachusetts, so that I could use the library archives for my historical research on the roles of American women. We were renting one of those dignified Victorian clapboard houses laced with stairways and window seats. Jeanette cooked, read, sang, sewed. One-year-old Becky crawled and shouted and chased the cat. Four-year-old Benjamin tricycled briskly up and down the sidewalk. And I spent mornings in a room at the far corner of the third floor, smoking my pipe, reading Berryman and Creeley and Sexton, and then scribbling my own poems. Afternoons I rode with Benjamin on the trolleys, visiting a soda-bottling factory, a museum, or the Charles River. Or I went out alone with my camera and then down to the basement where I had arranged a rough-and-ready darkroom. Evenings, after my wife put the children to bed and I kissed them goodnight, the two of us sat with friends in the tiny yard, shielded from Shepard Street by a bamboo fence, and we talked, smoked marijuana, danced to Jefferson Airplane and Iron Butterfly, ate Brigham's ice cream.

Only in July, a month after we arrived, did I open up the cardboard carton in the corner of that third-floor room. There they were: five gray-and-white-marbled rectangular boxes neatly lined with hundreds of five-by-seven index cards on which I had scribbled two years of research notes. It was time to get back to business, to take a fresh pack of index cards down to the Schlesinger Library on the History of Women in America and resume work on my second book. But still I left my watch on the shelf, smoked dope in the evenings, wrote poems on the weekends.

In one of those poems I met a high school friend:

> Furtive as spies converging on a busy street,
> you and I negotiate recognitions
> beneath small talk: you a gentle moustache,
> wife, three trim children, a career;
> I much the same, minus moustache.

I wanted to remind him of how we used to help each other with algebra problems before school, and how we murmured about the girls we loved that week, and how we hooked swish shots every afternoon.

But my tongue
turns coward when you wink
without my tears, shake hands, and carry off
your family, moustache, career.
I lurch into the gear of my thirties,
heart twitching with the treason.

The small gestures of that Cambridge summer seemed so large
to me because until then I had worked so hard, so desperately
hard, for so long. For three years I had worked as a history teacher
at the University of North Carolina. For two years before that, I
had worked as a history teacher at Lincoln University. For five
years before that, I had worked as a history student at Harvard.
For four years before that, I had worked as a history major at
Swarthmore. For six years before that, I had worked as a student
at Manhattan Friends Seminary, and before that at P.S. 135.

This is what they call a "vita." But a vita is not a life.

I cannot remember a time before I was reading. I can barely remember a time before I was in school. When I look back, a few scenes
flicker against my memory's screen.

The New York Public Library. Every Saturday morning I tuck the
four books under my arm, ride the 42nd Street crosstown bus,
and walk between those two stern stone lions, past the guard with
his silver clicker-counter in his palm, through the marble hallways
echoing gently, and down to the Children's Room. I signed my
first library card at the age of five, large letters that dipped embarrassingly below the line while my mother and the librarian smiled
upon me. And almost every week since then, I check out four
new books. Dog books, horse books, orange-bound books about
heroes and heroines, undersea and in-the-air books, Hardy Boys
and Bobbsey Twins. Certain favorites—*Lou Gehrig: Boy of the Sandlots,*
and *My Friend Flicka*—I have read five or eight times.

My Father's Office. Riding the elevator up to the seventeenth floor,
surrounded by the damp rough overcoats of businessmen and secretaries, I feel small. Across the rippled glass door, "New England
Mutual Life Insurance Co." is stenciled with dignity. Then the
sounds of the business world rush at me: the clacking typewriters,
the buzzing switchboard, the chattering calculators, and the water

fountain belching. I am awed by the way my father talks on the phone, thrilled by the respect that his colleagues and secretaries give him. On each visit I ask him to explain again what he does, what an "underwriter" is, and each time I can't understand most of it.

Roller Skating. In the middle of New York City a kid can't have a bicycle; that would be suicide. I have roller skates instead. On Sunday mornings I quietly pick up my skates, hang the skate key on its gray string around my neck, and go down to the street. At this hour on Sunday even New York is serene. A last turn with the key, until I can feel the metal clasp pushing through the shoe against my toes. A tug on my gloves. A check of my coat buttons. And I am off, rrr-rrr, rrr-rrrr, my eight ball-bearing wheels charging into the cold quiet morning, rrr-rrr, down to Second Avenue, up to 44th, across Third, watch for that subway grate, down Lexington on the smooth asphalt, gliding now, a quick glance for cops and then through the door and into Grand Central Station, rushing along the tiled floor almost frictionless, almost fantastic floating, the grinding of these eight wheels along the stone corridors wrapping me inside a cyclone of sound. A few pedestrians stare, smile, snarl, but I whizz past them, untouchable, omnipotent, the fabulous mysterious long-distance skater of Sunday mornings. I skate for miles before I go home to Rice Krispies and toast. Sometimes the bottoms of my feet tingle until lunch.

Sentences. Beyond the half-open living room door my mother confides to an aunt that, "according to his I.Q. score, Peter is a genius."

After the school bell rings on the last day, my sixth-grade teacher summons me to her desk: "I want you to come back and visit me when you become President of the United States."

In the eighth grade, at the height of my fervor as a Yankees fan, my mother casually remarks that "of course you won't become a major league baseball player." My Phil Rizzuto dream explodes, I'm morose for weeks.

School gradually becomes work. I did everything my teachers asked me to do, and I did it early. I went to Sunday afternoon movies only if I had finished my homework for Monday morning. I read the Sunday *Times* before Tuesday in order to meet with Jed and

Michelle in the weekly Current Events Club and discuss Joseph McCarthy (whom we opposed) and Negroes in the South (whom we favored) and the Korean War (I can't remember how we stood on that). After school I played basketball on the cement court until the anxiety in my chest rose too high and I took the IRT express home to do algebra before dinner, history and French after dinner.

During the eleventh grade, while walking alone one night along the East River, I decided to become a teacher of history. The decision did not emerge from agonized questioning back and forth. It simply arrived intact, as an image of myself: I was conducting a classroom of students (like Toscanini in front of the NBC Orchestra), with the huge movements of past wisdom and events cascading in the space between my students' minds and my fingertips. It was an absolutely clear image, and absolutely convincing.

In the end I ranked second in my class of twenty-five, behind Michelle and ahead of Jed. Solemnly I listened to the graduation speaker, solemnly marched in step with "Pomp and Circumstance" down the aisle, and three yards from the door an incredible "Ya-hooo" broke from my throat and I leaped into the summer night toward the champagne party, the all-night dancing, the pre-dawn voyage very merry back and forth on the Staten Island Ferry, and the wide hug of my future.

And hug me it did. Swarthmore College was everything I had expected, but more gloriously so. I worked for the student newspaper, joined the creative writing club, knocked on Philadelphia doors for Adlai Stevenson. I pondered the obscurities of the Introductory Philosophy text until my head gratifyingly hurt. At "rush time" I joined the debate between the fraternity faction and the bohemian faction, and chose the bohemians. I hummed along at folk concerts on the lawn and pounded my fist on the Symphony Hall bench in unison with Shostakovitch's Fifth. I borrowed a pipe from my father and learned to smoke without feeling dizzy. I fell in love and fell in love again and then for part of freshman year was in love with two girls who happened to be roommates. I could not imagine being happier than among these brilliant, creative, thousand students and teachers clustered on this little campus eleven miles southwest of Philadelphia in 1956.

During the next three years I focused my energies especially on studying. The farther I traveled into the field of history, the larger it became, the more enormous my decision to "be a historian," so I lowered my head and read all the more furiously.

In junior year I began to date Jeanette, warmed by her smile and gentleness, engaged by her intelligence, and gradually—month by month—reassured by the sense of our stability. I threw my imagination forward ten or twenty years and there we were, conversing or embracing or reading, grayer and plumper, but otherwise unchanged and unchanging. One afternoon Jeanette talked about studying in Europe for a year after graduation. "You mean, you would go off and leave me?" I asked plaintively. "Not forever," she replied, as her hand closed around mine, "just for a while. I love you, but I also want to see Europe." My heart pounded with apprehension which grew during the next weeks into a panic that I could hardly bear. Finally I asked her to marry me, and repeated the proposal until she accepted. We both applied to graduate school, and when I won a fellowship to the Harvard Ph.D. program, she accepted an offer from the Harvard School of Education master's program.

The spring of 1960 was a season of ceremonies. Commencement. Wedding. And also the annual Swarthmore poetry contest. Slumped in my auditorium seat as Robert Lowell announced the winner, I heard my name and pulled the collar of my brown leather jacket above my ears as if. . . . As if what? I wasn't sure. My brain locked—silent and immobilized. Robert Lowell, the poet whose work I had admired above all poets, had chosen my poem out of all those poems and said my name aloud to my friends and teachers. But no "Yahooo" answered in my head. Only this frozen silence, which was a way of saying . . . what? Two or three days later I figured it out. Lowell was telling me to keep on with my poetry, but I had already told myself that in graduate school I would probably have to defer poetry or even forfeit it. I was refusing Robert Lowell! Yet what alternative did I have? After all, if I was going to become a historian and a husband, then. . . .

The prize-wining poem said it all too clearly and sadly.

COMING OF AGE (May 1960)

> I first walked in shoes of metaphor
> (a fantastic conceit, perhaps,
> and yet I once dared more)

past the boys with blue felt caps
scuffing head-bent to Sunday school.
I leaped into waves of knee-high grass,
tumbled over shadows and played the fool,
disrupting a grasshoppers' dancing class.
Fancies tickled my inner eye.
The sun rolled upwards on the sky.

I climbed a tree toward that light,
hung at the hub of a wheel of birds
circling in ecstatic flight.
Within me worked a flurry of words
anxious for form, for the solution
of absolutes. I hung in quarrel
with myself, undoing all that I had done
and remaking it as before, to no avail—
a weaver working with one thread.

The sun's heat bristled upon my head.
I jumped, listened for the hearts of hills
(if hills have hearts, which I knew then
and still believe). But distant bells
gossiped, tower to tower, in the town
where men lived between walls and doors,
where stone and glass and polished steel
divided and divided the air. My pores
gaped with panic. I ran, fell,
and yielded to the sun's demand. I came
to water the flowers in my dusky room.

I have become a man among men,
must take a position and name it.
I own a public syntax, a fountain pen
to sign my name, to communicate
with those who never listen for
the distant pulsing hills. And I hold secret
my heart's adventure
from their careful wit,
while startling head-bent passers-by
with a sudden whistle and eccentric eye.

Harvard was awe. Widener was the biggest library of them all. My professors were big names who seemed beyond my reach as they lectured from podiums, typed behind frosted-glass office doors, or chatted stiffly at four o'clock sherry parties (or was I listening stiffly as they chatted graciously?). This was the big league and I felt medium-sized, Rizzuto beside Mantle.

No doubt, many of my fellow students felt equally awed and diminished, but I don't know that very certainly because I didn't dare confess my insecurities. I barricaded my jeopardy within a fortress of labor. Awake at eight, bike to class at nine, bag lunch from twelve to one, library until five, bike home, dinner six to seven, study till ten, then read a novel or listen to music or make love. There were so many books to read, so many centuries to master, so many theories to unravel—too many, too many. "They wouldn't have accepted you if you couldn't make it," I reminded myself. "You can do it," Jeanette said and said again when I turned to her for comfort.

I needed to know that I was needed. I needed to make a mark. On a bitterly cold January afternoon I trudged to the commons room of the Law School and stood among a hundred others before the television set where John F. Kennedy proclaimed "the torch has been passed to a new generation of Americans." In the *New York Times* that I bought each morning at the Harvard Square kiosk, I read about sit-ins and freedom rides, pickets and boycotts. One balmy April evening, I sat amid hundreds of people in the Emerson Hall classroom where I had listened for a semester to Oscar Handlin's brilliant, monotone lectures on social history. But tonight we were hearing other professors and applauding their shrill, sometimes profane phrases, because yesterday Kennedy had ordered the invasion of Cuba through the Bay of Pigs. In my living room at midnight I sat beside the telephone, trembling because I had had the audacity to send a telegram reprimanding the president of the United States.

And then there was H. Stuart Hughes's campaign for the Senate. This courtly, somewhat abstracted professor of European intellectual history, who had lectured grandly to us on Durkheim and Croce and Keynes, who was fluent in French and Italian and German, had decided to campaign against Kennedy's younger brother, Ted, in the name of disarmament and socialism. Hughes inspired me and puzzled me. I handed out leaflets and knocked on doors and stuffed envelopes with evangelical zeal; this was the politics of high principle. But when Hughes spoke to midday shoppers in Central Square, his long sentences curling among the pizza aromas, or when his horn-rimmed glasses reflected the white T-shirts of factory workers in Worcester, he seemed pitifully, almost comically out of place. I felt uncomfortable for my teacher and crusader.

Well, then, where should I go instead? In 1962, instincts and conscience pointed me down Blue Hill Avenue into the ghetto.

When Dick and Gretchen mentioned their work with CORE, the Congress of Racial Equality, I was immediately interested. The next Wednesday Jeannette and I squeezed into the back seat of their Volkswagen and we drove down Mass. Ave., across the river, under the elevated MTA tracks, down Blue Hill Avenue, the evening turning dark around us, the faces turning dark, past row upon row of three-story houses and storefronts until we arrived at a large church in the middle of Roxbury. For the next two hours we sat on wooden folding chairs in a circle of fifteen people, mostly white, mostly in their twenties, all well-spoken and middle class. But this was not another academic seminar. They were talking about job discrimination, rats, segregated schools, hostile city councilmen and cooperative ministers, rent strikes, picketing. Conditions one could see, people one could touch, actions one could do. Through this little circle I glimpsed the real world. Through it I felt the surge of grand principles: justice and equality.

Jeanette soon stopped going to CORE meetings; somewhat shamefully (in the face of my righteousness) she preferred singing Bach and Brahms with the Harvard Memorial Church choir. But I had no hesitations. Even though I would have to work all the harder to make up for the lost study time, I proudly signed my membership card and pinned on my shirt the black button with the white "=" in the center. In CORE I could make history, not just study it.

Wednesday evenings: reports, arguments, votes, laughter. Saturday afternoons: knocking on scuffed doors in Washington Park, asking for signatures on petitions against urban renewal plans ("urban renewal means Negro removal"). Tuesday afternoons or Thursday evenings: going out with one or another apartment-seeking family to "test" landlords for racial discrimination. And one September week in 1963, marching outside the office of a Dorchester realtor with cardboard signs ("Equal Treatment for All"; "Black and White Together"), singing slave spirituals to taunting Irish bystanders ("we shall not be, we shall not be moved") and then, on the climactic afternoon of that week, the three of us walking as planned into the realtor's office and sitting until the crowds came and the reporters came and the police, and three officers gripped our arms and led us into the van and the station and the cement cell. All night I felt heroic and frightened. The next day, in my living room, I glimpsed myself on the front page of the *Record American:* the sleeve of my brown tweed suit rumpled in the policeman's fist, my face flat white, my eyes invisible behind the flashbulb's glare on my horn-rimmed glasses. I looked young, frightened, out of place, like . . . yes, now I see the resemblance . . . like a youthful Stuart Hughes! But I never saw it then.

Flowing alongside the lives of graduate school and social action, there was also home life. Jeanette and I rented a two-room apartment three stories above Dana Street. The floorboards creaked, some windows didn't open and others didn't quite shut, the hallway ceiling leaked a bit during heavy storms. But it was our first real home together, so all creaks and leaks were forgiven. At 5:30 P.M. I unlocked the door and used my briefcase to block Pippin, our surly cat, from galloping down the stairs into the basement (at least once a week he out-maneuvered me, emerging hours later in sooty triumph). As I sat in the kitchen while Jeanette cooked a casserole and told about her eighth graders' escapades and I told about my day's work and a Mozart divertimento poured from the hi-fi, my face went warm with congratulation. She is so pretty; we love each other well; we never argue; someday we will have children; we are succeeding. And I kissed her after dessert before I went to my desk to study.

But always I held something in reserve. Occasionally, as we talked in bed at night, she said: "I feel as if there's some mysterious part of you that I don't know," and I nodded in reply. I protected the "mystery," put it into my diary, into my poems and stories and the first ten pages of an unwritten novel, and into those Humphrey Bogart/Dylan Thomas/Albert Camus cigarettes I smoked broodingly alone at midnight. I believed it was some future exultant epiphany that I sheltered inside my silence. But also down there at the bottom of this "mystery" lay fear—unmentionable fear, because if I confessed to Jeanette how afraid I was of failing school, failing my artistic self-image, failing my future, I would thereby default on the promises I had made to her and my parents and her parents and my teachers and the rest of the world-in-waiting. And then where would I be? Where would I go? I had a map in my head, like those maps my father obtained before a vacation trip on which the American Automobile Association had marked "the best route" in wide red ink, and I couldn't imagine how to travel without it.

"I really wish you would reconsider, Peter." We were sitting in the Harvard Faculty Club, where my dissertation adviser, Frank Freidel, had invited me to lunch shortly after I had completed the manuscript. Surrounded by more Ph.D.'s, Pulitzer Prize winners, and Nobel Prize recipients per square yard than any other place in America, I was having a little trouble concentrating on our conversation.

"This is the best year for jobs that I can ever remember," Freidel was saying. "Stanford, Oberlin, perhaps Michigan, you can almost take your pick. I just don't think you'll be happy in some second-rate college. Believe me, I've taught in some. I admire your idealism, wanting to teach in a Negro school, but I think you're making a mistake."

He said it kindly. I had chosen to work under Freidel because, of all the professors in the history department, he seemed the most humane. And he was. In fact, until now he had never criticized me. But this afternoon, to my astonishment, he was upset by my decision to join the Woodrow Wilson Internship Program and teach at a Negro college.

"You see, Peter," he added emphatically, "we at Harvard produce some of the leading historians in the country. You will leave here and go on to shape the future of the profession."

He had never spoken this way to me, and I felt confused. "All I can tell you is that I think I'm making the right choice." I chewed the last piece of the veal parmagian. "And if I'm wrong, I can always apply to Stanford later." And meanwhile I would send my dissertation to Harvard Press, a bit of career insurance.

What I did not say to Freidel, because I did not fully say it to myself, was that I wanted to keep a healthy distance from the dynamo of Harvard and places like it. After five years amid the high-powered whir of the Big Time, I needed to step back for fear of being mangled. I said nothing like that because it sounded like personal weakness. And in any case I had impersonal reasons that formed justification enough. In this tear-gas season of Selma, I was going to teach black college students, helping the brightest of them go on to the best graduate schools and enjoy the same opportunities for success that whites like me had had. (The very opportunities that I found menacing and wanted to escape! The paradox jumps at me now, but I didn't notice it then.)

As it turned out, I did not go south, but west—to Jefferson City, Missouri—and to a university that was not all-black but half-black and half-white—Lincoln University. In almost every other respect, however, the next two years matched my hopes.

The chalk squealed as I printed my name on the blackboard. Next to "PETER" my shoulder blades had left moist circles where I leaned back, oh so casually, waiting for the bell. Eighty faces out there attending me. Would my voice come out as a whisper or a roar? But it came out as a voice, and then everything was all right. More than all right, it was wonderful. I was teaching history—the ten-year-old dream come true. Puritans, slaves, Sons of Liberty, Federalists. . . . Week by week I brought them back from the dead and set them moving to the questions of my mind. Why did the colonists come? Why did Nat Turner rebel? Would you have joined him? What if the British had won? Was the war worth it? Which side are you on, boy, which side are you on? Those thousands of inert monographs and periodicals, facts and dates, were finally coming to life, kicking up curiosity and argument and sometimes laughter in my students' minds.

During the first months I would listen over my shoulder for the advice of Professors Handlin, Hughes, and the others. But Cambridge was a thousand miles away. I was on my own, duly licensed with a Ph.D. to practice my craft. Moreover, at Lincoln University my Swarthmore-Harvard pedigree dazzled all eyes, even when I uttered banalities and botched discussions. Perhaps I had found "the best route" after all, which was off the four-lane career highway and onto the secondary roads where I could not so easily fail.

At six o'clock I drove into the carport, sat at the kitchen table and pulled off my tie. "We're having meat loaf tonight," Jeanette said with a hug. I spooned spinach into Benjamin's mouth, steering between his propeller arms. "He said 'Ga' at the cat this morning," she announced while setting the table, "and he stood up for almost thirty seconds." To distract him while we ate dinner, I turned on *Sgt. Pepper's Lonely Hearts Club Band*. It was the eighth complete Beatles performance that day, Jeanette told me, but Benjamin's love affair with the album was insatiable. At 10:30 I came up from my basement study, reasonably pleased with my lecture for the morning class. Jeanette and I drank a beer, chatted about the George Eliot novel she was reading, checked the baby, and went to bed.

Everything was in place. But Jefferson City was not our place. One movie house, usually featuring Doris Day or Walt Disney. One book store, the American Freedom Bookstore run by local John Birchers. One main street, which rose grandly past the dome of the state capitol building and then scurried among used-car lots, vanilla-custard stands, and billboards until it opened into the fields and aimed unswervingly toward Kansas City.

If it was hard to fail here, it was also hard to know whether I was succeeding. In 1967 we turned eastward. Harvard Press had published my dissertation, I had begun work on a second book, I had been offered a job at the University of North Carolina. It was time to move. Yes, but time to move on or move back or move up? As yet I did not fully know the meaning of my motion. At most I knew that I was moving up into a first-class academic institution, though not moving back within mangling range of the Ivy League dynamo. But that was all I knew. From some remote interior place a muffled voice urged: "More." But as I drove our green Chevy II over the Smoky Mountains, I could make no sense of what my heart was trying to tell me.

The message assembled in fragments and disguises during the next three years, like clues in some enormous treasure hunt. "Cancer is the growth of madness denied," wrote Norman Mailer toward the end of *An American Dream*, the novel with which I brought to a climax my course on recent American history. Pacing back and forth across the classroom already thick with the heat of North Carolina summer, my jeans clinging to my thighs, my denim shirt open, I fervently explained Mailer's existentialism. Walk the edge of violence and you approach orgasm and perhaps love and perhaps sainthood. Travel into the desert and perhaps you can make the long-distance connection to the golden girl in heaven.

"Either you're on the bus or you're off the bus." The next year it was Ken Kesey and his dayglo Pranksters who ended my course. "We all are watching a movie of our lives, a split-second lag behind reality. We must overcome the lag. We must live immediately."

And then other messages arrived, from the body rather than the head. "Come on, baby, light my fire," wailed Jim Morrison and the Doors. I turned up the volume and danced alone in our living room until sweat rolled under my clenched eyelids. For fifteen years I had pushed my feet in the humiliating corrugated-cardboard steps of Miss Harris's Wednesday-afternoon class. Now at last my body could hear the beat, and I danced for hours to the Stones, the Doors, and Dylan.

The air of the late 60s swarmed with messages, like the car radio when you drive late at night across the countryside. My friend Jed, in his senior year, sent back his draft card and awaited jail. My friend Charles left school to work as a labor organizer because "the university has lost its legitimacy for me." Arnie, Jeanette's younger brother, had attended graduate school in history but suddenly left all that to live in a commune and publish an underground newspaper. On Christmas Eve I sat across from Jeanette in the living room, glossy red and green packages all around us, and said, "You know, Leonard Woolf once wrote that everyone should change occupations every seven years. What if I changed?"

Meanwhile the old momentum continued. I covered hundreds of index cards with notes on hundreds of articles and books that were supposed to blend someday in a book about women's roles in modern America. I was promoted and given tenure. I won an award for excellence in teaching. Becky was born. Everything was in its proper place, but where in hell was I going?

It was now, in the summer of 1969, that I went to Cambridge and laid my wrist watch on the shelf. The time had come for choosing. Either/or! Scholarship or poetry. Work or art. Liberal institutions or radical alternatives. Tenure or adventure. Either you're off the bus or on the bus. I was prepared to make fateful choices.

But June became July, July became August, and somehow either/or continually melted into each other. From nine to five I typed index cards at the Schlesinger Library, wrote poems on weekends. Walking among the painted, acid-tripping, grass-dreaming crowds at the Sunday rock concerts, I took black-and-white photographs. One morning I rode the bus alone to Providence to visit Arnie and his commune; three days of talking, listening to music, selling the newspaper to shoppers on the Mall, getting high on hash at Stuart's place and walking home through the cool city dawn chewing hot rolls bought from white-aproned bakers whose shop materialized magically on a side street that I could never find again . . . and on the third day I rode the bus out of Providence back to where I had begun.

Nevertheless, choices were gradually being made. I did not see that fact because I misunderstood not only how I would go about choosing, but also what was up for choice in the first place.

Late in August, Jeanette and I sat in our little yard with Carol and John, another couple from Chapel Hill. Within a week we would all be back there, classes would resume, the momentum rolled on. I was telling about Arnie's commune when Carol interrupted, "Hey, let's do something like that. Our two families could buy a house together, share the cooking and child care. Damn! What an adventure!" I leaned forward and felt the muscles of my thighs twitch under my palms. John cleared his throat, "Well, I don't know. . . ." "Oh, John!" she broke in, waving her cigarette. "For God's sake, it's time we took a chance." I tried to catch Jeanette's eye but she was looking down at her feet with an expression I couldn't read. "Peter what do *you* say?" Carol touched my wrist. I drew a breath, which emerged as a laugh, "Sure, what the hell."

When we sold the house one year later, Carol and John had separated and were planning to divorce, Jeanette and I had separated and were planning to divorce, Carol and I were in love and planning . . . well, our plans were not too clear, except to live in passion and poverty. Inside that white clapboard house, events and emotions had accelerated beyond what any of us could keep up with, until the centrifugal force had thrown us out and away.

Soon after we moved in, I wanted to repaint the chocolate-brown bathroom—or rather, I wanted all of us to repaint the bathroom. If we were a commune, let's work in common. The other adults were not particularly interested, but the kids were. So on Saturday morning Becky, Benjamin, Ellen, and Ray (aged one to six), and I took off our shoes, put on old clothes, opened half-gallon cans of blue and orange and yellow and green, and began to paint. Thirty minutes later we had done the job. Stripes, circles, faces, trees, peace symbols—it was the goddamdest one-and-only-looking bathroom in the entire state of North Carolina, and I couldn't stop laughing as we rubbed the turpentine between our blue, orange, yellow, and green toes.

One morning Jeanette and Carol and I were having another of our discussions at the breakfast table. Carol was saying, "But how else will the poor or the blacks get attention unless they make trouble, disturb the peace?" She flicked the ash of her cigarette into an egg cup. "And it's up to us privileged people to help them." And Jeanette said, "That is what I've always admired about Peter, the way he. . . ." And I cut her off, "We're not talking about me, Jen, so stop changing the subject." And almost before I had finished, Carol came at me in a fury, "I can't believe you shut her up that way. So contemptuous! If ever you do that to me, I'll slap you." I stared into Carol's blazing eyes, bewildered and thrilled.

One evening as Crosby, Stills, and Nash filled the house with their harmonies, I took Becky's pudgy little body between my hands and whirled around the living room, the two of us giggling louder and louder. But by then—three or four months into the commune, two or three months after Carol and I had fallen in love—every pleasure moved against an undertow. "Dance with me, Jen," I said, but she shook her head and kept ironing. "Why are you ruining my fun?" I said. Between the hisses of the iron she said, "Why are you being so silly, dancing and giggling like that?"

Everything had a way of turning upon itself. "Love" became a weapon, and then a wound that would not heal. "Commune" became four adults circling and colliding and recircling. I said "self-actualization" and John replied "self-ishness" and Carol said "being open" and Jeanette replied "being mindless" and too soon someone began the next round. I had never felt such pain and never such ecstasy. Some days I felt that I was breaking apart into jagged pieces. Other days I felt that I was soaring full of joy.

In the end we could no longer contain the centrifugal force of ourselves and split into four. Abruptly the future opened wider than I had ever seen it. Incredibly I was entering a second life. Instead of "lurching into the gear of my thirties" as a traitor to youthful hopes of blending work with love, here I was at the age of thirty-one speeding into the dreams of my poems. To be sure, along the way I had snubbed Jeanette's generous loving and patronized her pain. I had violated her trust and John's. I had put Benjamin and Becky aside. But I could not contemplate that now. All I could think was that at last I was breaking the sticky bind of either/or. Goodbye index cards, goodbye marriage, goodbye heavy, oh so heavy, success. But somehow nothing happened that way.

"Sometimes I wonder if I'm ever gonna make it home again." It was the year of Carole King's *Tapestry* album. It was the summer when Carol visited a commune in upstate New York. After a month without letters or phone calls, I knew she would not come back. We used to talk about running away together; now I must learn to be my own traveling companion.

Girding myself to leave the academic world, I spent the summer in New Haven working at a youth crisis center. A flock of free-flying folks passed through: teenage runaways; thirty-five-year-old Ph.D.'s living on federal grants and in borrowed apartments; an Israeli hitchhiking around the world. Toward August I found myself looking forward to teaching in my classroom at Carolina. Surprise!

More surprising yet, while working night shift at the crisis center, I spent a month of afternoons at Yale University's library writing a chapter of my book. But I did not sit there stooped under that feeling of duty like at the Schlesinger Library and so many other libraries of my life. It was not the same feeling; it was not the same book. For years I had been listening to women learn and teach the lessons of feminism—how men had oppressed them, and how women had collaborated or succumbed. Slowly, very grudgingly, I had begun to acknowledge my own part in this drama of inequality, and slowly I had planned to do penance in my book. But in 1970 I had an abrupt insight; my book was only half a book, because a study of sex roles must talk about women *and men.* My enterprise, once professional and then also feminist, became a personal quest, too. I was asking not only about "them," but about us, about myself.

"Sometimes I wonder if I'm ever gonna make it home again." I had left a marriage which I considered too narrow for my emotions, and soon I felt achingly homesick. At one A.M. I rehearsed phone calls to Jeanette that would end with us happily reunited, words I never believed but wanted to. Halfway through a tepid afternoon I daydreamed of singing Becky to sleep, watching *Leave It to Beaver*

reruns with Benjamin, soaping their sleek bodies in the bath—
those homely enjoyments I had neglected. I bit my lips, pounded
the sofa, and sobbed.

Coward! In the motionless heat of my New Haven apartment
I berated myself. What but fear holds you back from rebellion?
Walk into the desert! When August ended and I drove down the
New Jersey Turnpike toward Chapel Hill I felt, more helplessly
than ever, a traitor.

IS THIS THE FORM MY WISDOM TAKES?

There must be a proportion to things,
no less tonight in the drench of dark.
Parrots, you know, sleep so secretively
that even they don't know when.
In my own case, I thought about you
until you grew too small to be recognized.
There must be many such cases on record.
Actually, I find I know less each year
of whatever it is I predicted.
In the end, they'll say, age cleaned out his mind
except for those things he really lived for.
All possibilities are proportioned to belief.
In any case, I'll keep jogging down this beach
and watch for you in the morning.

In 1973 I wrote my last poem and greeted the silence with considerable sadness and relief. Yes, relief—which perplexed me, because
for half a lifetime I had made poetry the holy grail of my secret
journey. But, no doubt about it, prosaic silence brought relief.
At first I couldn't understand why. Then I realized that I had had
the same feeling, the same lifting of pressure from the back of
my eyes, when I had stopped civil rights work. And come to think
of it, I had felt similarly relieved when I did not run away with
Carol and had instead returned to Chapel Hill and my children.
What did these three activities have in common? Each offered a
form of heroism—an aesthetic, a political, and a familial form. Yes,
that would explain why I surrendered them with relief; after all,
heroism is a heavy business. Apparently I was, then, what I had

accused myself of being: a less-than-hero, a coward back pedaling from heroic futures.

But something still was unexplained, another emotional connection that was even more puzzling. I felt the same relief in canceling the heroisms as when I stopped writing my sex-roles book for the historical profession and began writing it for myself. This "new" book hardly constituted cowardice, though. On the contrary, it felt more like an assertion of self, an act of fidelity to what I wanted rather than what others expected. "Well, then," I said quizzically to myself, "Turn the argument around and take a second look at that so-called heroism."

Poetry and CORE and elopement were heroic, all right, but more precisely they were heroic rebellion against the other half of my life, which was career and marriage. I was waging an inner civil war: heroism versus success. But whichever half won, I would lose. *Either* equaled *or*. In the desperate effort to escape my need for conventional success, I had reached for anticonventional success, which simply reversed the equation and left me under the same burden. Poetry, civil rights, and Carol were "the best route" run backwards. I had betrayed myself twice—once in success and again in heroism. The crime was not to have worked so hard, but to have worked toward expectations not my own. The crime was not to have sought escape, but to have fled toward goals not my own.

But if not toward "success," what then?

April 1979. A year has passed since I wrote the preceding pages. A year ago I answered my "what then?" with two final jubilant pages which told how I had harmonized all the parts of my life. In the last paragraph, I jogged alongside my new wife into the sun-bright future. A year ago I thought I had written the end of my essay.

I was fooling myself. Oh God, was I fooling myself! I so urgently wanted the end of the essay to mark the end of my confusions about achievement and work and happiness and love. Or to put it another way: I so urgently wanted to come out as a success. But a year later, as crisis has once again overtaken me, I realize I haven't yet come to terms with my dilemma. Whatever my hopes or my needs, I won't end this essay with triumphant answers. No success here. No failure, either. Just an attempt to address myself with honesty.

In 1973 I began to arrange my life along more settled lines. Benjamin and Becky were living in Chapel Hill with Jeanette and her new husband. At least twice a week the kids visited me for an afternoon and dinner, and on alternate weekends they slept overnight. We were very crowded in my two-room apartment, but crowded also meant close, and our closeness warmed me. On a typical day we ate spaghetti for dinner, brownies for dessert, watched the Sonny and Cher show, told another sequel to our endless goodnight saga about the friendly dragon, and at midnight I listened gratefully to their rhythmic breathings of the darkness. Since then they have grown toward teenagehood with astonishing speed. Their lives have filled with braces, disco music, track practice and piano practice and viola practice, with Benjamin's endless baseball discussions and Becky's sleepless slumber parties. Each year they delight me more.

In 1973 I was also falling in love with a woman named Kathy. She was a student in my course on American women's history, a feminist, a psychology major, and a poet. Beautiful, brilliant, aloof Kathy. After graduation she planned to live alone on Martha's Vineyard, writing poetry and walking the winter beaches. She was never going to marry. She was following a vision that led her from a small farm in eastern Carolina to the university at Chapel Hill and from there toward some destiny that glowed like the Hollywood she always wanted to visit. After several intense conversations over coffee and a kiss in the middle of a spring afternoon, I fell in love with Kathy. During the next six years we wooed each other, lived with each other, and then married when the word "marriage" seemed unlikely to freeze us.

In this second marriage I was determined to break the patterns of the first. A partnership of equals—that was our watchword. At first we divided the bills in half, even separating her long-distance phone calls from mine, until we decided that fifty-fifty was unfair; after all, her earnings as a waitress or later a secretary hardly matched mine as a teacher. I did most of the cooking, except for her southern specialties of potato salad and barbecued chicken. She, with her eye for arrangement just askew of bland symmetry, tended the furniture, plants, and her umpteen dozen wicker baskets. I made photographs, she wrote poems and stories, and we trusted each other as critics of our art. I played harmonica to her guitar when she sang Joni Mitchell songs with fierce beauty. I had my friends, she had her friends, and some friends we shared. She drove her yellow Ford to Greensboro where she studied for a master's degree in creative writing. I drove my black Volvo to Chapel Hill where I taught my history classes. For six years I was profoundly, sometimes incredulously, happy with her.

Parenthood, marriage, teaching, cooking, photography—loving and working—I had found everything I wanted, and yet . . . and yet something was not right. For months I was content and then, without warning, I passed into a time zone where I felt something was awry, something I could not quite name. The worst phase occurred when the history department was evaluating me for promotion to the rank of full professor. I became irritable with Kathy, awoke at five A.M., loudly said I didn't care about promotion, while inside me a nagging voice said, "You don't deserve it. If they only knew the 'real me,' they would expose you as a fraud." When the department voted against me, I squelched the dim spasms of anger inside my chest, and decided to try harder to earn approval next year. Another phase came when I finished the book on sex roles. I fantasized about bestsellerdom, television appearances, and royalties rolling in like an avalanche of chocolate chip cookies. But at the same time my mouth turned dry with the memory of those dusty, tedious library hours, and I vowed I would never write another academic book. I would do something fresh, creative. Photography? Multimedia productions? Cooking? I tried and enjoyed them all, and yet I never seemed to find fulfillment in any of them. The best part of my life was loving Kathy.

And so it went—I went—for six years, until everything came undone.

> The time has come—say it
> goddamn say it out—
> my father died last June
> leaving space,
> leaving space
> where I may claim myself
> no one's son but mine:
> his last deed of bringing up,
> my first and most brave.

I wrote this poem at the beginning of 1979, as my life began to come apart. Kathy went to an artists' colony for four months, where she had won a fellowship to write. Alone at home, I dove furiously into various projects I wanted to complete, only to discover that I kept colliding with an invisible barricade. I wanted to write some stories, wanted to work on photographs, but could not, mysteriously and absolutely could not. And meanwhile I heard ominous sounds in Kathy's letters and phone calls: "I'm realizing I have for years wanted to be on my own like this." "I feel like a new person." "I see now that I have stood behind you, let you protect me." "I am so happy tending all day to myself and my writing and nothing else."

Two months after they diagnosed the cancer in his lung, my father died. Three months after leaving, Kathy wrote that she wanted a divorce. As I type these sentences, my throat closes with aching and anger. Tears swim across my eyes. My mind still lurches for a moment before acknowledging what has happened.

I have been thrown back upon myself. I live in the wide space that these two departures have opened. Through dreams and poems and emotional sessions with my therapist, I have begun to understand what I did not understand before. During most of my life I have been pursuing the kind of success that my father taught me; I have traveled "the best route" toward seriousness and security. Poetry, playfulness, and photography, by contrast, were tangents that merited no "real" respect. So my father believed, and so he judged me, and I worked desperately hard to reverse the judgment and win his approval. But I could never really win, because his approval never covered all parts of who I am. The harder I worked, the fiercer my sense of apology. Oh, what a vicious circle! I didn't see it until now, and therefore didn't see how to escape it. I must learn to approve myself. Only then will I stop looking ahead toward goals that are not my own. Or come to think of it, maybe the point is to stop looking ahead and start living more fully where I am here and now.

I suspect a similar pattern in my relationship with Kathy, although the wound of her leaving still hurts too much for me to be sure of what I know. She too remained just slightly out of reach, an ice queen whom I dreamed to thaw with my passion and my understanding. Again and again in those six years I would tell her, "I love you well." And in many ways I did—with respect, gentleness, laughter, protectiveness. Looking back, however, I perceive a flaw; unconsciously I was trying to succeed in love as in work. I was trying to win from Kathy the approval I could never win from my father. I had made our relationship a kind of vocation.

My father has gone, and Kathy has gone. The external structures have broken, the internal ones are exposed. Lurching into the gears of my forties, I am left to learn how not to betray myself. I carry with me all the givens of my past—the ones that drag me down to pain, the ones that propel me with imagination. I carry all my givens, my gifts. This essay ends at the edge of wide open space.

5
Scenes on the Way to a Plateau

by Robert Hahn

April, 1965, a Friday afternoon. Nicky and I are driving in a white VW convertible with the top down, passing a bottle of Fix beer between us, rolling free. We skirt Mt. Parnassos and go by Thermopylae and make a straight track through the plain of Thessaly. Sunlight falls on the green wheat like a blessing. We are joyous.

English teachers from the American Community School, off on our spring vacation, we are headed for Meteora and its monasteries built on pinnacles of rock.

Life is simple for us. Married for four years, we have no children yet. We both teach full time, and we work hard, zealots about preparing our classes and correcting our papers. But we play hard too. We go out with our cronies, we close down *tavernas*. We build fires on the beaches at night and picnic in the ruins by day.

We reach Meteora at sunset, winding up to a cliff which looks out on the monasteries. On a sheer ledge still warm from the day, we drink ouzo and eat cheese and olives. A breeze comes up from the plain, ruffling our hair, and in our exhilarated state it seems the rock where we sit is slightly stirred. But everything balances.

Indiana, 1950, walking home from school with Freddy Unsworth, a fellow sixth grader. Today is the end of a marking period. Trudging along with a hard-bitten smile and a card full of D's, Freddy is going to catch hell. He seems fearless. I don't flaunt my own A's, for in fact I am in awe of Freddy's reckless courting of failure. I would never dare.

One of my earliest memories is listening to Jack Benny on the radio. I liked him better than Sky King or The Shadow, because he was funny, and because his humor emerged from a slight exaggeration of the adult world. Benny was always harried. His problems, never very pressing, often stemmed from mismanagement of simple chores and logistics. I don't remember what he did to earn the money he was so tight-fisted about, and I doubt if I knew then. But I think I sensed that what gave the humor its flavor was Jack Benny's aversion to adulthood. He didn't want to grow up. That, and not simply fear of aging, was the clue to his vanity about the blue of his eyes (not their luster, but their innocence), and his refusal to pass beyond the threshold of thirty-nine.

That was a quarter century ago, and I have just turned thirty-nine. I am like Jack Benny in other ways as well. I have spent years learning to write poems, but now my poetry reminds me of Benny's violin playing.

Benny seemed to feel that life was making demands on him that he didn't want to meet. Here we differ, somewhat. I've been following a comfortable, one-track career as a teacher, and I have tenure, but a changing job market has convinced me it is wise to look for new training and a new credential. I'm on my way back to school to earn a doctorate, planning to spend the second half of my work life in administration, and if this means more responsibility, more stress, more demands, that sounds good to me. I've grown bored with my teaching, and I need a change.

But I do have ambivalent feelings about the threshold of thirty-nine, and in my case as in Benny's, these feelings have roots in the child's ambivalence about entering adulthood at all. Some of us never outgrow a certain reluctance; at the same time, mindful of the rewards that adult reality advertises, we are always eager for its advent. For example:

Get a job. Get married. Get on with it. At the tag end of the Fifties, a young man with the right antennae heard those messages everywhere. When I drove in from New Jersey to meet a girl beneath the clock at the Biltmore, they sang overhead, leaping from tower to tower. When I drove the other way, the messages followed, swooping through the tunnels of the Pennsylvania Turnpike and onto the flatlands of Ohio, greeting me morning and evening as I crossed Tappan Square at Oberlin College. Oberlin's motto was *learning and labor.* I understood this to be a rephrasing of the same message. One was meant to work hard, make the dean's list, and get a job. Getting married, by some weird but irresistible logic, was part of this process.

I sympathized with Charley Starkweather, a Kansas teenager who went on a shooting spree because the alternatives were killing him. Charley saw that grown-up life was a bore, and he couldn't adjust. For my part, I read *Time* and bought the whole package. I couldn't wait. I hurried. I arranged to become a married wage-earning adult within a month of my last undergraduate final. No cross-country trek with a boyhood chum, no world tour, wild oats, nothing. Bang. Here is how it happened.

The discovery of adult fiction, around the eighth grade, was my discovery of reality. I think it started with *Knock On Any Door* by Willard Motley. Something in its mix of style and plot and tragic mood struck me as more real than anything in my own experience, and this response made me an ideal audience for several theatrical high school English teachers. The lights went up and the show was on. Ahab and Hamlet spoke to me, E. E. Cummings and Dylan Thomas sang their tunes. This was the life.

When my senior year at Oberlin began to draw close, I decided

I was likely to find no pleasanter occupation than mounting the same production for other young people. I would teach. I took education courses (when no one else I knew would go near them), practice-taught, and became (strange word) "certified" so that I could begin without delay. Now:

Nicky and I had been having an affair for a couple of years. I thought she was brilliant and beautiful, and we were good friends. We liked to fool around together. We enjoyed the same things, we shared a taste for bed and literature, and when we were cast as Stephen and Molly in a production of *Ulysses in Nighttown,* it seemed perfect. Shouldn't we get married?

Nicky transferred to Swarthmore. I followed her east, and after we were legally joined in a ceremony we both professed to despise, I started teaching in a Philadelphia high school. What a rush. We set up house in an apartment over a delicatessen with a neon sign that blinked BARBEQUE CHICKEN 99¢ all night in red. The message seeped in our windows along with the growl of trucks downshifting for the stoplight at the corner. In the mornings I put on a tie and walked to work swinging my briefcase. It was February 1961. Adult life had begun.

November, 1975, dark falling fast as the faculty meeting moves into its second hour. I have just been elected chairman of the Faculty Senate. It reminds me of playing Monopoly: You have just been elected Chairman of the Board, pay each player $25. But this is real enough, I suppose. It gives me an exercise of responsibility outside the classroom, and I enjoy that. Later in the year, when the college is torn by internal strife, I will have some interesting problems to solve. But I won't assume the chair until next month, and today's meeting has grown trivial and boring, as perhaps only faculty meetings can. I daydream out the window. The parking lot dissolves into a football field, the Giants have the ball, it is third and short yardage. I fake a handoff, drop back, set, and fire. The pass is complete for a first down.

A Saturday in January, The Present, and the whole family is home. Kids seem to fill the house, though there are only two: Charley, going on twelve, who wants to play professional basketball when he grows up, and Sarah, nearly nine, who means to be an archeologist or a magician. Nicky and I have to work, as we usually do. She's finishing her dissertation, I'm drafting a syllabus. By now we have a co-equal marriage, so that in the morning I am on call for the kids, and in the afternoon we switch. Things get done. I make dinner while she sorts the laundry, and at night we work again.

I think of a cartoon by Goren: a couple at a cocktail party holding up their end of the conversation. They are hairy and squat, they look as if they just came out of a cave. Each has an arm slung over the other's shoulders. On their faces are strange, crazed smiles, and one of them says, "Our marriage works because we *make* it work!"

Eastern Flight 842 climbed briskly into the sky over Columbia, South Carolina, and headed north. Just as briskly, all business, I set aside the view and bent to a clipboard, making notes. By the time we circled down to Hartford, I had a sketch of certain approaches to my professional future, a second career, and this sketch, in time, led to my plan to return to graduate school and enter administration. That was not why I had gone to Columbia.

Four years earlier Nicky and I had made a deal. She saw no future in English teaching, and she wanted to go to graduate school in Criminal Justice.

A fine idea, I said. Go. I'll do the cooking, I'll pay the rent, I'll tend the kids. When you finish, I continued, you'll be able to get a good teaching appointment in a university, which is more than I can be sure of myself.

Right, said she, and added, then I'll support *you*, and you can write full time.

Terrific, I answered. I'll resign my teaching job when that time comes. We'll sell the house and move wherever your new job takes us.

We shook hands.

We went to our respective corners of the house, and four years later Nicky was flying here and there for interviews. Offers came in. The University of South Carolina. Did we want to live in the south? Iced tea and grits? In *South* Carolina? I flew to Columbia on a reconnaissance detail. Ostensibly I was there to get a feel for the place, to check out housing and schools for the kids. I did, but it proved to be irrelevant.

By the time I boarded the return flight, I knew that I simply didn't want to do it. Following Nicky to Columbia would mean abandoning an independent professional base, and would mean committing myself indefinitely to the role of writer-in-residence in my own house. In a sense, I would be alone, all my psychic funds invested in an introspective, scribbling life, and my only lifeline to the world a string of magazine publications, and reviews, if there ever were any, of my books. I felt I would be lost.

As Jack Benny would say: Well! Here was the chance every writer craves, and I wouldn't take it. I remembered the quizzical looks I had seen on friends' faces whenever I described our deal. They seemed to be asking, But what would I be giving up? And for what? Why? I had to go to Columbia to ask myself the same questions.

When I came back I had the answers. I understood that I needed the conventional certainties and supports of a profession, a position. This, apparently, was who I was. The recognition was refreshing.

Fortunately, Nicky had other offers, and she settled on one in Boston. We both had jobs we wanted, and the family was together on weekends.

When I'm fifty, will my decision look like a resolute move or a slump of resignation? How should I know? One of the things everyone in our family seems to enjoy these days is the Museum of Fine Arts. There is a huge Gauguin which I love, for its mysterious, dreamed quality, and its surprising title. It is called "Where Do We Come From, Who Are We, Where Are We Going?"

A summer morning, any summer in my early thirties, and I am fretting over a problem in the architecture of a long poem. The third section is crucial to my stresses and balances, but its metaphor doesn't correspond to the rest of my imagery. If I let it go, the reader may find this a bold stroke, disdaining surface coherence to discover unity at a deeper level. Then again, the reader may not.

An elm outside my window has been tagged by the town for removal, and into the middle of my problem comes the tree surgeon with his hydraulic lift, his saws, and his crew. By afternoon he is ready to top-off. This involves cutting off the limbs beyond the reach of the lift. Girdled in leather and hooked to long ropes, he balances in the highest fork, wielding his chainsaw like a broadsword, and each time a limb falls, his perch recoils and shudders. He doesn't blink.

"Now," I say to myself, "now that's a man! Now that's work!" When I ask him to cut the limbs to fireplace length, I feel he is looking straight through me.

Later, through the chances of a small town, I get to know his wife and she takes me into her confidence. In her eyes, the man is an alcoholic disaster, insecure, childish, cruel in petty ways. I don't know how he feels about her. They are separated now.

What I've said about jumping straight from college into marriage and work is only part of the story. It is true that I was doomed to be a premature solid citizen, but I had a shadow life too. I was a poet.

A girlfriend at Oberlin gave me a brilliant birthday present: inside a shoe box, a bottle of gin and a copy of Rimbaud's *Season in Hell*. Here, surely, was a symbol of what I was meant to do, deliberately derange my senses and practice my craft.

I did a lot of both as the years went on. Rimbaud as a model gave way to Yeats, and Yeats to Stevens and Williams. I wrote in the evening whenever I had a chance. In the summers I wrote all morning and half the night as well. When a new idea was coming or an old draft shaping up, I felt that this was the most interesting and satisfying work in the world. I still feel that way.

I appeared in magazines, but for years it seemed I would never publish a book. Then the miracle occurred, followed by another. But these longed-for events, once the blessed objects had gathered dust on the coffee table, brought with them a chilling knowledge. The poems were all right. But all in all, really, they weren't that good, and if the recognition I dreamed of was out of the question, who could say this wasn't perfectly just?

I don't know how clear-sighted a man can be about the sources of his own failures. Regarding my limitations as a poet, I suspect the roots are to be found in a need to keep up the appearances of respectable adulthood. If some of us are reluctant about growing up, some of us (and we may be the same people) are also reluctant about giving way to the anarchic emotions of childhood; the furies and the passions, the love, the pure playfulness, the joy. To succeed as an artist is, in part, to succeed in remaining a child. A man who succeeds in this way has to run some risk of failure as an adult. Looking out from the midlife plateau, I can see how well I have protected myself against this risk.

In retrospect: marriage

After a while wedding anniversaries are like New Years Eves—you try not to overreact—but we did go out for our seventeenth. The Orson Welles was running the new Cacoyannis film of *Iphigenia* (there's a work/family conflict for you), so we saw that, and then we went to a Greek restaurant and drank retsina and ate stuffed grape leaves. As usual we saw different things in the film, but it was interesting to talk about it. A low-keyed evening, much like the marriage itself.

Nevertheless, what Lawrence says about relationships (in *The Rainbow* and *Women in Love*) seems perfectly true to me. A true relationship is a terrible struggle of wills. We must fight to preserve (to discover?) our individuality, our selfhood, and we must labor to lose it too. Union (coming through?) has nothing to do with the sappy "togetherness" of the Fifties, or the liberal pieties of Kahlil Gibran and his branching tree (read at our wedding ceremony); it is a battle to the death of something.

The observable history of my marriage, of course, is generally less intense than all that. But it is a checkered history, with periods of closeness and phrases of estrangement, with other people in the picture, with legatos and largos of the monogamous sublime relieved by shifts in the rhythm, exuberant moments when anything could happen and sometimes did. I will say that the cost of an "open marriage" strikes me as high, and the emotional dangers great enough to make one suspect all glib generalizations on the subject. But I must say, too, that the sense of having *lived,* of having experienced some of life directly is, to me, worth the cost.

My marriage in retrospect looks like an antic mixture of modes, an opera, a happening: we've been drinking buddies, bed mates, diligent members of a mutual-aid society, and much, much more! For a marriage is not, after all, only one version of a long-term relationship, but, also, an arrangement in which the needs, obligations, jobs, earnings, identities, and roles of two people get sorted out.

Which brings us to the subject of feminism. In our early years (having fled the apartment with its barbeque chicken sign, for Cambridge first, then for Greece, then back to Connecticut), our marriage was stolidly conventional in its division of labor and assignment of roles. That is, it promoted the man and abased the woman.

For many of us, the Sixties, however evanescent, were in fact a time of enlightenment. For those of us who had grown up not only absurd but naive and stupid in the narcoleptic Fifties, the later decade was a time to learn about capitalism, about racism, and, alas, about the sexist structure of one's own life.

It is painful to recall those years when I was teaching at a girls' prep school in Connecticut and Nicky was raising our first child. Chagrin! While I sat on the greensward chatting with young ladies about John Donne, my wife (that's right) contended with a two-year-old's temper, oh, she cleaned, she shopped, she cooked and made beds and kept records of where I'd sent my poems. I would spare myself the pain of this memory were it not that many otherwise bright people see nothing wrong with such an arrangement, provided it is "chosen" by the woman, which is like choosing a lobotomy.

We had, in other words, a storybook marriage.

It takes a while for consciousness-raising to produce changes in structure. For example, even when our children were old enough for daycare and both Nicky and I were teaching in a small college in western Massachusetts, even then, yes, I was full time and she was part time; I was the respected professional, and she was the woman, the wife, the mother, the parttimer hired because she was on the spot. Our credentials and education were identical.

So we got the message. If Nicky's activist feminism sometimes angered me (when, for example, it laid at my doorstep—because I was male—blame for problems which hardly began at home), still, we perceived the same problem, and something, we agreed, had to be done. By the time she went back to graduate school, I had learned how to manage a house and take care of two kids and handle a full-time job, all at once. It is hard, but it is a lot easier than being just a housewife, a role not fit for man or beast.

Finding a way to solve (at least in our own lives) the societal problem of sexism has proved to be one of the best experiences of my life, and it has gone far—along with the shared sense of humor and the general camaraderie—toward making sense of this strange legal arrangement called marriage.

One of the monasteries of Meteora is still active, if undermanned, and in fine repair. The entrance to its chapel is frescoed with a wrathful God presiding at the Last Judgment, where sinners spill down to the jaws of monsters and the instruments of torturers. Rising before daybreak, shivering with devotion and cold, the monks pray for strength. They must be strong to resist the temptations of joy.

In retrospect: children

I have had children for more than a decade now, and with one of them almost twelve and about to vanish into the fog of adolescence, the experience begins to round itself off and take on a certain finished quality. On the whole, I've loved being a parent, although the role has sometimes been at odds with other and more immediately gratifying or beguiling ones. One of my poems deals with such conflicts. It is called "Wallet."

> So the talk turns
> to kids, teeth, cost
> of schools/You have
> kids? I have pictures look
> here where your head
> swings over the bed's edge singing
> strange tongues your legs
> straddle air & your
> hands gripped under your thighs what
> balance! Here
> you're on top/Had you
> practiced that
> gait for years to be
> barely grounded

between your thighs riding
up
& down as if I
were a cloud and you
really ought
to see my kids

Since I have started quoting myself I will go on with a poem in
which my son Charley makes a very early appearance:

Creation is celebrated here
I hate to be sentimental
but at such times I think of my children, of
Charley waddling with buckets in his hands
one red, one blue, both full of air
& the only word he knew was o.k.

. . . and I will conclude with my most shameless father-daughter
love poem:

Here goes Sarah The Poem Rated X for
you at age six, I grab the sled
& shoot it down the hill, you
fly on your belly arms spread
knees bent & your boots
sticking up, red suit blue sled & black-on-white
trees going by, a drift at the
bottom, watch out, the cold
hits your face & colored lights
start to dance in the
hearth, apple logs glowing where melting snow
is brushed from your cheeks
a towel in your hair, you smile at him
sideways, your robe, watch out
falling partly open, leaning back
on your elbows, bare feet to the
fire I've made
burn low, afternoon's last light

brought through the curtains
to brood on your thighs, your breath
speeding up entwined with a handsome

stranger who has saved you, so this
is what happened when you never
came back, when the blue sled

vanished in the soft white
drift O Rosebud, Sarah, who
was that masked man I saw you with

Well. My children, really, have played a great part in my life and it seems only fair to give them a decent share in this account, but what can I say? They are growing up! I love them madly, and I'm glad they could take time from their busy schedules to join us here on the show tonight.

"When I was a child, I spake as a child, I understood as a child, I thought as a child: but when I became a man, I put away childish things."

If one wants an antithesis to Jack Benny, St. Paul is a good choice. I also have early memories of Paul. His rhythms and imagery appealed to me strongly, and like Benny, he helped me see what growing up was all about. Paul is the great prophet of adulthood, the apostle of self-denial and delayed gratification. The idea is to plan well, avoid distractions, and work hard. For this, Paul says, the reward is heaven, but one should not be misled by his metaphor. The rewards are status, power, and money.

While I doubt that my intended new career will reward me much in these ways, my decisions have been suspiciously like those of a man who heeds Paul's counsel and justifies Wordsworth's pessimism:

Why with such earnest pains dost thou provoke
The years to bring the inevitable yoke,
Thus blindly with thy blessedness at strife?
Full soon thy soul shall have her earthly freight,
And custom lie upon thee with a weight,
Heavy as frost, and deep almost as life!

May, 1978, driving to work, and a sweet drive it is, slicing through a stand of pines, looping down by an apple orchard, and running past a row of old maples in the valley; a drive I have made for nearly a decade, from the rambling house half of which is now mine and half still the bank's, to a college where the curriculum by now bears the imprint of a few of my own initiatives; a drive that can make the heart leap up and fill the eye with joy in all weathers. Today, a sign says CAUTION: MEN WORKING IN TREES. As I come into the valley, there they are, yes, men working in trees! men by the thousands, thick as a flock of migrating birds, little men at tiny desks. Maples full of men bent over their work, leafing through papers. They are all wearing suits. They all have my face.

6
Only Connect

by Tom Kreilkamp

Some brief background about me will help place this essay in context. I was born in 1941 (and on writing this, am thirty-seven). I
am the oldest child in a large family of eight children and was
raised for the most part in the middle west of America. My father
taught philosophy, my mother English. I came east to school on
a scholarship to Exeter when I was fifteen, and then went to Harvard. While there I met Vera (who was going to Wellesley), married
her at twenty-one, went to New York City with her to graduate
school, she in English at City University, I in psychology at New
York University. In 1967 we returned to Boston where we have

105

lived since. I first taught psychology to undergraduates at the University of Massachusetts/Boston for eight years. I then turned to what I am doing now: therapy and psychological testing with children, at McLean Hospital, a private mental hospital in the Boston suburbs. We live in Cambridge with our two children, both boys, aged ten and five.

All of this provides some sketchy coordinates. In what follows, I will refer to one or another of these briefly stated biographical facts in an attempt to point out what I see as their significance. Others I will ignore, even though they are not trivial, because they do not form part of my topic, or because I am not sure what to make of them. For example, the fact that we have been married sixteen years is at one level hard for us to believe (it does not of course seem that long). At another (sociological) level, it probably hints at something deeply atypical about us which may disqualify everything I say from having any general pertinence. Any two people who are so out of touch with contemporary social reality as to stay married must be . . . etc. What do we know about anything? Perhaps we're pathologically stubborn (I said I'd do it, and by God, I will). Perhaps we never really communicate enough to get divorced. Who knows?

Most of this essay will attempt to focus on, or move around, the topics of work and family: how do I attempt to connect the two, and with what results? I will not say much about my own "career" (college, graduate school, teaching, therapy, writing a book) except as it bears on my attempts to balance the kind of concerns inherent in "having" a career with "having" a family. For this is not a curriculum vitae but something different. It is a discussion of the process and purposes of my life. And the central theme will be "success," or rather, my effort to redefine success.

I am a first-born son, and my parents were ambitious for their children. They never pushed me toward any particular career, but they raised me with a belief in hard work and the importance of doing well. Of course, they raised me with much else besides, part of which will be reflected in this essay as I struggle to analyze my efforts to combine work and family life without sacrificing either one to the other. My parents clearly gave me the psychological wherewithal—in some mysterious sense—to engage in the struggle I am caught up in; another set of parents would have made any such attempt much more difficult.

What is the struggle? There are two parts to it. The first takes place within myself, as I reflect, analyze, and argue myself hither and yon, trying to figure out new meanings for the old word "success." I am clearly out of sympathy with the old conventional standards of success, although I was raised by them. The old standards meant getting good grades in school; they meant being well behaved; and they meant being concerned about finding a career which would give me not only a sense of something important that needs doing, but also some form of external rewards.

All of this now seems somewhat meretricious to me. And yet, just as women may tell themselves that raising a family and being a homemaker is not a very high standard of success, yet withal often find themselves thinking and feeling in terms of the old standard even while striving for a new and better one, I similarly find myself drawn toward the old standard in spite of myself. There is an unresolved conflict here and I am not at all sure that resolving it is going to be possible.

A considerable portion of my conflict here is connected with my experiences of being raised as a male in a culture which values certain kinds of male achievements. The world of sports, for example, epitomizes a realm of achievement which many American males find very appealing, even compelling. An aspect of this world of sports is, of course, winning and losing. In the sports realm, who wins and who loses is rather clear, and this clarity is quite attractive. There is also a large concern with the "best" in this world, and much of my own up-bringing, in which a covert yet powerful concern with being best was inculcated, is now evoked for me by my ten-year-old son who constantly talks of the "best." He is an avid reader of the *Guinness Book of World Records.* I am a child psychologist and I have an understanding of the way in which this kind of concern is appropriate for someone his age.* But to some extent, I have never outgrown this kind of concern. As a child psychologist who is interested in human development, I can see that this situation represents a fixation in my development. I am stuck at a stage which I should have grown through a while ago. But as an American male, I find this altogether normal. That is, my joy in keeping up with current statistics on the "best" in professional baseball

---

*I do not know whether girls his age are equally interested in the *Guinness Book of World Records.* In my experience, they are not, but my experience is sadly limited and I know of no research on this topic.

is something that joins me to my ten-year-old son, and to countless other men (and some women of course) in my culture. Is this not as it should be? NO!! But what can I do about it? Precious little but struggle.

And struggle is what I do. But the way I struggle is not by inveighing against the publication of the *Guinness Book of World Records*. Certainly the book is tied in with the success-achievement nexus which provides the ambiance in which so many men live and die. Certainly, too, it is silly. But people who know that do not need to be lectured about it, and people who do not are unlikely to cease conducting at least part of their mental life in "record-making" terms even if all copies of the book are burned. So do not bother to attack that book. But do try and understand what underlies the fascination with that book which is so much a part of the ten-year-old boy culture in America and, to some degree, the male American culture. That is what I tell myself as I conduct my internal argument about "success."

My struggle contains another part, which bulks much larger in my life, and that is the daily effort to work out a life which will enable me to share with my living companions the burdens not just of diapers and dishes but of money and success. And this is the truly grueling part, because it has almost no ground rules and few guidelines.

The problems here are innumerable. Some of them are connected with the difficulty of living with anyone different. I did not marry someone just like me; we share some standards but not all, and working out together what we believe in is an on-going process. Some of these problems arise out of complexity, and much of that complexity is ordained by our choosing to live in a city, by choosing to have children, by choosing to work outside the house for much of each day. But some of that complexity is connected with the larger contemporary difficulty: the lack of a clearly articulated set of rules for relations, within marriage, between the sexes. What should a man do and be? This problem has emerged as women have taken the trouble to articulate their own questions about the nature of their lives. Every time a woman wonders whether she should have to wash the dishes, a man living with that woman must ask the same question.

I happen to be with a woman who has never thought that she should have to wash the dishes. This arises not out of a current devotion to feminism, but out of what I see as a kind of self-respect. Not that washing dishes is so bad, but that she is committed to sharing the burdens of homemaking and child rearing, and this commitment arises out of her own feeling that she deserves a wider sphere. Thus she has never had much difficulty in insisting that I share the work at home. On my side, I was raised doing housework. Because there were eight children and much to be done, our parents encouraged us to help, or even demanded that we help, and I fell in with these demands. Not that I did not fight them as a child, but, in some deeper way, these demands came to seem perfectly reasonable to me, so that now I find myself doing dishes with no feeling of being forced to do something unmanly, something obnoxious. I do not exactly enjoy it, but I see the task as necessary. Thus Vera and I both believe in sharing the housework.

Nevertheless, our negotiations about who does what and when are rarely easy or even susceptible of solution. Sometimes we both feel that we have more important work and we both wish this world of housework and child care would evaporate. We often live in a house that many would consider less than clean (both our mothers, for example, would probably find our housekeeping standards somewhat below theirs). We do not always eat a traditional meal and instead make do with cheese, crackers, omelettes, and odds and ends. The only reason this works at all is because neither of us overwhelmingly minds this situation. Sometimes, of course, sexually conditioned attitudes get involved in our disputes over such matters. For example, my standards for cleanliness in the house are lower than Vera's. I do not feel the condition of the house reflects on me in any important way. Vera feels it does reflect on her; and in a deeper way, she feels depressed when things are messy for too many days in a row, whereas I do not.

The issues arising out of care of the children are more complicated (in our case, at any rate). We both are very much committed to caring for them. We have different notions of what constitutes proper care, of course, as any two people (from our fragmented society) will. Every issue here is potentially a battleground. What should Jacob eat for dinner? What chores should Ivan be required to do? Which clothes are appropriate for a birthday party? When is a child so sick that he must stay home from school? All of these are trivial issues when two people agree on some fundamentals;

but when people do not agree, all of them can turn into arguments or worse.

Our fights occur in part because we each care about other things as well. These other things may be connected with our careers, or they may arise out of our respective desires to "get away" into some other realm (of freedom from household cares? of pleasure and enjoyment?). And this latter desire can only arise out of a kind of self-respect, assuming one has grown beyond sheer self-centered indulgence which arises out of an inability to make any commitment and an insensitivity to others. This is a complicated issue which women have long since begun discussing, but which men have not really gotten to yet, since for men the dimensions of life are too often work versus play. Women have the considerable advantage of living within a different mundane structure. Insofar as women live part of their lives outside the career-ambition-money-earning nexus, they are accustomed to doing things not for money, but for some other purpose. They thereby enjoy a tremendous freedom from a certain form of dominion. Of course, they then suffer, correspondingly, from other forms of constraint, and perhaps from a lack of self-respect. But they are less likely to condemn themselves for not working for money. For a man, or at least for me, that represents a raised consciousness which is not easily maintained.

I have come to recognize two difficulties in our fights over how to share the labor. One is that we do not agree on what needs to be done, or when. The other is that we each feel involved in these matters, and neither of us can shrug and say, you decide. Role division may be regressive, according to contemporary mores (in our small circles), but it does have some important benefits; for example the man or woman can leave certain decisions to the other, and the other can make them without feeling hampered by having to consider another's opinion. This is a tremendous savings of psychological energy. But in our case, we forfeit the savings because we both get involved in the decisions.

The question about appropriate birthday clothes is troublesome but hardly as big as the question of who stays home when the children are sick. That question, in turn, leads to the still bigger one of whose work is more important and that final question is one we have never really solved. At best we have devised different *ad hoc* ways of coping with it.

For years both Vera and I taught to earn money, staggering our teaching schedules (with the cooperation of our respective institutions) so that on any given day, most of the time, one of us could stay home with a sick child and not have to cancel classes. At one point, I was working part time; at another, Vera was working part time. At one point, I was not working at all. During these variations in our work life outside the home, the one who was more "at home" would stay with the sick child.

But two years ago I took a regular full-time job, which requires that I be out of the house five days a week, usually from 8:30 to 6:00, sometimes longer (not much longer, but sometimes till 7:00). This is not, by the standards of many of my male peers, a very demanding work schedule. But it is enough to make life in a family difficult. I cannot conveniently take off when a child is sick, though I can and do when it is necessary (and in fact right now, as I type this, I am with a sick child, having cancelled my appointments, while Vera has left for her teaching). Similarly, Vera does not like to cancel classes when a child is sick, though she will if she absolutely has to. What we have been doing lately, therefore, is to arrange a patchwork quilt of "coverage" by other people for such emergencies. Twice in the past two years, my mother has responded to our call for help and come to take care of sick children for a week at a time. For lesser illnesses we have hired people to help out at home with the children. These solutions sound easier than they are; to find these people, to keep them, to arrange for their illnesses as well as ours and those of the children, is an energy-draining process. Because Vera does most of it, she feels the burden more than I do. We are now in the third year of this current situation—both of us working full time outside the house—and the only conclusion I can draw from the experience is that it is terribly difficult to manage.

After my current job commitment is finished, I would like to avoid working full time outside the house until the children are older. I have work I can do at home—writing and reading—and I would prefer to avoid any commitments which would require that I be out of the house five days a week. This decision is not easy, because it is hooked into my earlier topic, success. I have no doubt that any kind of limitation that one places on his working life entails some curtailment of career. There are certain jobs which I simply will not pursue, demanding jobs which might give me more responsibility and more challenge and more "career opportunity" (as it is called). Similarly I have for years avoided looking for interesting jobs outside our present area, because we have both agreed that we like living where we are and because any kind of move connected with my getting a better job would most likely entail Vera's losing her job and not being able to find another comparable one. This last is by no means certain, but very probable, given the nature of our training and credentials. I happened to pursue a Ph.D. in psychology which is more marketable, as it were, than the Ph.D. she pursued in English literature.

But this "happened" is very crucial, since my "happening" to pursue psychology when I was twenty years old was in part a function of my thinking in terms of earning a living, and this kind of thought was related to my being a male in a culture where men are expected to earn a living. And Vera's happening to pursue English literature is related in turn to her not worrying extensively about "earning a living" and that in turn is related to her being a woman in our culture. Other factors enter, to be sure: in the early 1960s when we both were finishing college and thinking of "careers," English literature still seemed an economically viable degree. Ultimately, however, I believe that historical circumstance weighed less than sexual conditioning. For example, Vera has never finished her degree, and I finished mine years ago. I did this not because she was supporting me, but even as I was earning a living. She did not do hers partly because of her temperament, partly because the historical circumstances changed, but in part also I am convinced because, as a woman, having such a degree in hand did not seem so important. Ultimately she thinks in terms of my supporting the family. This is true even when she is (as she has been for years) earning money. And we have tremendous fights when I argue that if I share in dishwashing, I ought to merely "share" in money earning. I ought to have equal responsibility for earning money, but not to feel that I should earn more. She objects, arguing that I can earn more than she (given my degree and training, this is true) and therefore ought to do so.

And this is the rub. When I argue that I want only to work part time, so that I can be flexible in determining what hours and days I will spend at home, and thus share in more of the homemaking work, Vera objects, not because she objects to this goal, but because she thinks (correctly) that it will limit my earning power.

She does not mind that I do not seek a "better" job elsewhere, since she does not want to move, but I suspect that, in her heart, she would like me to have such an interest, so that I would conform better to her tacit image of what a "good man" ought to be. This image is not, I think, one she is proud of, or one that she accepts with the liberated portion of herself, but it is nonetheless there and active.

My not looking for jobs outside this area, my not going away to conferences, my not working in the evenings, my not subjecting the household to the dominion of my work or career-dictated needs is not simply my commitment to my family life. Part of it is—for want of a better word—laziness. In order to live this way I must, at some level, have renounced certain forms of ambition which, in our culture, are typically found among men of my background. I went to Exeter first, then Harvard. Most of my college classmates and friends have pursued careers of one sort or another. My parents both went to graduate school. In short, my background has placed me in a social world where people have career ambitions for themselves. These people, to be sure, include men as well as women. But the men in particular seem to be ruled by these passions. And as a man I have been struggling with particular intensity to get free of those passions, partly for the sake of a loving life with my family, and partly out of what I called laziness.

Another word might be skepticism about the value of fame and money and other attendant rewards of a successful career. Work and family have been for me relatively easy to balance, in part because I am not intensely ambitious. I have no desire to rise to the top of my profession. Nor did I have any desire while in college to rise to the top of my class. I did not want to flunk out of college, of course, which I suppose is a kind of ambition, but certainly not a very elevated desire. I am not obsessed with being best, though saying why would not be easy. Part of the answer lies in the fact that my life has exposed me to a number of people who are regarded as "best" at something or another, and on meeting them I have never found that they were to be envied. They would have one thing—respect and fame—but not many other things which seemed vital to me. If I had not known these people early (after I came east to school) then I might perhaps have nourished hopes of being one of the best and eventually attaining some brighter sphere of living. But I found out that the best were not the brightest and were tarnished in many ways, and so I did not lust for their lives.

Another side of this issue is the real possibility that my lack of interest in earning more money, or in becoming better known in my field, is connected with my interest in sharing in family and housework. (It is also related to other less benign aspects of my personality, of the sort that psychoanalysis uncovers.) Of course, there is no rule stating that this need be the case, but in my case these different strands seem to be woven together. That is, I am less interested than many men of my background in having a good career; I am more interested in helping with the family; and I think the two are somehow connected.

But part of my lack of ambition is, in addition, a defeatism, a passivity, a skepticism about all effort, and this rubs Vera the wrong way. Not that she is more ambitious than I. But she does to some degree live through my accomplishments, and if I had more of the conventional ones she would feel better. And here is an enduring source of conflict which is intimately connected with the division in sex roles in contemporary America. For women more often than men expect to live through their mate's achievements. In Vera's case, this is ludicrous on the face of it, since her attainments in college, for example, were considerably greater than mine so far as grades went. And this fact—that Vera to some degree lives through my accomplishments, minor though they are—is in turn connected to the larger complex topic of our attraction for each other.

Understanding attraction between a man and a woman, of the sort which leads to commitment (in whatever form), and the establishing of a family, is not easy. But since we all—in our generation, and that of our children too, I believe—have grown up in an era and a country where sex roles are differentiated, there is a real possibility that our attraction for another—in my case, my attraction to and for a woman—arises out of and is to some degree rooted in this kind of sexual differentiation. If this is the case, then my attraction to my wife may be contingent on her being womanly in some manner (the fact that I cannot state what that manner is does not mean it is not there). And similarly, if she is attracted enough to me to love me on a lasting basis, then she may expect me to be male in a variety of ways—sexually, economically, sociologically—and thus any attempt to change the definitions of masculinity and femininity may to some degree intrude on this attraction. This line of thought may be misguided. I am honestly unsure of its merits, either in my own case or in the general case. But the whole issue concerns me because I have discovered that in my own fight to emancipate myself to some small degree from the dictates of conventional masculinity, Vera is far from being a consistent support. Thus although she likes having me help her do housework, and in fact, insists, and although she expects me to share in the child care, she does not expect herself to share equally in the money earning, and she expects me to do more than my equal share in pursuing a career. In fact, she does earn as much money as I do right now, but she does not expect to go on doing so, and she certainly expects me to earn more than she does.

Another way of approaching the same problem is as follows. Women want to be released from the burdens of nurturance. They argue that men should not rely so much on women for support and "help" in their "important" life work. This makes sense to me. But in my own case, I notice that along with this effort to diminish my own reliance on traditional femininity goes a constant struggle about a related but different set of ideals, those which surround the idea of masculinity. Men are often asked—I certainly am—to be strong, to appear unworried and in control, to be calm, to make decisions, etc.—even while they are asked to forego the old conventional supports provided by the old ideals of femininity. That is, they are asked to remain "masculine" in some ways (for the sake of the women), and yet to decrease their reliance on women. There is something askew here. Why should women be allowed to shuck the feminine roles and men be forced to stay with the masculine roles?

Although Vera and I have worked out a *modus vivendi* so far as taking care of the house, earning money, paying the bills, relaxing, and having fun with the children, we are far from having worked through some of the fundamental issues involved in the changed life we are trying to lead. For example—and now I am getting to topics which stir me, which make me feel that there is much to be accomplished in terms of understanding how to construct a reasonable and enjoyable life—we have not really penetrated the complex issues behind her ambition to free herself from the role constraints inherent in being a conventional housewife. Those issues arise when not only she attempts to attain such freedom, but

I do as well. There are many expectations of men in our culture, and she is not happy when I abandon them. When I say "do it yourself" to her requests that I hammer a nail, fix a window, open a jar, dig a hole, or earn a living, she is threatened. The truth is that I have had much more practice in assimilating the ideology of contemporary female liberation than she has had in assimilating the as yet largely unformulated ideology of male liberation. Part of this imbalance comes from the accidents of our upbringing; my mother was more 'liberated' than her father. Thus my image of femininity (to take a simple-minded view of the derivatives of that image) has more scope than her image of masculinity. I expect women to have a lively intelligence, to be assertive, to earn money, and to be interested in the house and children. So I am not surprised to find Vera doing all of this. She expects a man to earn a living (as her father always did), to be both assertive at times and loving and kind and gentle at others (as her father was and is); but in addition, she has other expectations which derive more from her adult experience than from her childhood. That is, she expects me to wield a hammer (he never did), to vacuum (he never did), etc. And here the accidents, not of upbringing, but of contemporary history (in which female liberation has been a more important force than male liberation) are important.

Thus far I have been discussing problems which arise for me and Vera as we attempt to work out a way of living in which work and family are intertwined for both of us. But there are other problems consequent on my making family responsibilities as important as work responsibilities, and my attempting to develop that side of my personality which is connected with taking care of children and being nurturant. One set of problems is work-related. When I make clear that I have responsibilities to take care of my children, for example by bringing a child to work with me (as women sometimes must do), or by taking time off from work to go home to take care of a sick child, or to go to a school conference or assembly for one of our children, then my colleagues look askance. They may wonder what kind of commitment to my job I have, if I am willing to let these other tasks intrude on the work sphere. They may wonder what kind of wife I have, that I should be forced or allowed to do these things. They may feel implicitly criticized if I plead my fatherhood, for are they not fathers too, and am I suggesting that they are shirking their fatherly responsibilities when they do not behave as I do? We too have children, they say, and we don't have to leave work because of them; what's wrong with you that you do?

The other set of problems is connected with what women feel who see a man being nurturant, a man who is willing to serve coffee or who is good with children. This is a problem which has never arisen at home. Vera has never been remotely threatened by my ability to comfort a crying child or cook a dinner, any more than I have been by her ability to earn money and hold a job. But it is an issue, nonetheless, which arises for anyone who tries to act in a manner not entirely in accordance with the socially defined role.

Much of what I have been discussing in this essay can be seen as affecting identity and self-esteem. As an American male, I grew up with certain hopes, certain expectations, certain beliefs about the "right" way to live. To a considerable degree, I have been reworking these expectations, these beliefs, these ideas. Instead of believing that being "best" in a field is important, I have tried to move towards a conception of a life involving two very different endeavors, family and work, which have to be balanced to some degree. I have not tried integrating them, though I have had many fantasies about the kind of life a farmer might lead, where children and parents can work together, where family and work are intimately intertwined. I think the reason I have not tried to integrate them more, so that family and work were one and the same, is that I find considerable strength in the fact that they are separate. If things go badly at work, I can use my life in the family to recuperate; if things go badly at home, I can use work in the same way. If they were one and the same, such recuperation would be difficult. In addition, multiple perspectives are generated by having my feet in more than one place. Perhaps only a "modern" person would want his feet in more than one place, but just as I enjoy seeing other places and finding out about other ways of life, so do I enjoy having multiple perspectives to bring to bear on any given situation. And having my family—being a husband and a father, a cook and a dishwasher—provides me with a way of living which balances the life I have at work.

Of course the rewards of having a family are tremendous. I have not stressed them in this essay; here my focus has been on the problems inherent in working out connections between work and family. These problems did not really become intense until the children were born, and although the difficulties increased with the children, so did the pleasures. I have never enjoyed the house-work drudgery in and of itself, but the pleasures of taking care of children and watching them grow, and doing so with Vera, in-crease from year to year. And without these pleasures, the others—those consequent on my work and career—would seem meaning-less.

Thus there is a real sense in which having the family life gives me the strength to move out into the world of work, and in general, the movement back and forth from family to work has been easy. I should add that I am finding more tolerance at work now than I did ten years ago for my own involvement with my wife and children. Part of this change may derive from new general attitudes, but part is also a consequence of my moving from academic work to a hospital where I and my colleagues treat troubled children and their families. We see daily in our work the importance of involved fathers, of fathers who are concerned about their children and who do things for them. Thus we are each more tolerant, perhaps, of one another's attempts to give to our own children, to be a live figure in the domestic drama.

I have tried to make my self-esteem contingent not just on grades in school, or money earned on the job, but in my relations with others, and in a variety of endeavors, none of which pay money or further my career (reading, writing, doing volunteer political work, etc). What I want, ideally, is not to care too much about the end product—the big office, the large salary, or the beautiful child whom everyone else admires—but to care about the process, of working or child rearing. This is a tall order in a culture where end products are so highly valued. What is involved here, of course, is not so much that one is a man, but that one is a person in a materialistic culture, where there is no given hierarchy of values, where things are constantly changing. In such a situation, getting away from valuing what one has, or one's products, is difficult. And in a very general sense, this is what most preoccupies me; not my attempt as a man to integrate family and work, but my attempt as a person to forge a way of living which makes doing, of anything, as important as what one produces.

7
After the Scaffolding Came Down

from an interview with

Lawrence Rubin

People have criticized me for lacking clearly defined goals. I tell them that I prefer to play it by ear. Richness of experience—that has been my theme song and my greatest pleasure. At different times I have headed in different directions and entered different experiences. I have undergone success and failure and everything in the middle. Probably underneath it all, though, I have been going in one direction: the path to self-sufficiency, or at least the illusion of self-sufficiency.

After I gave up wanting to be a sports hero, I wanted to be a lawyer. This was in the mid-1950s. I was quite active in high school politics as a self-styled radical. I can't say whether that means anything or not, especially in view of the fact that I was also president of the student council. Could there have been a really radical student council president of 1956, amid McCarthyism and the foxtrot? Certainly my radicalism was not part of an organized political movement. Rather, it was a set of actions.

On Veterans Day, for example, I did not invite the traditional speaker from the American Legion, but showed a Quaker film entitled *Let's Give Grain, Not Arms, to the World*. That caused quite a stir in the school and community. One summer I went to work for the American Friends Service Committee on an Indian reservation near Bellingham, Washington. No one was required to wear neckties in school, so I wore a necktie every day. Of course at later periods of my life, when I was required to wear a necktie, I didn't. Sometimes I think the only principle of life that counts is perversity. I enjoy perversity. During those high school years I discovered some combination of radicalism and decadence that attracted me. Being a lawyer was somehow part of it. I was going to be the one who defended all the good causes against all the bad people.

I expected to go to college. There was no question about that. I was part of that large, competitive group that wanted to go to college, the bigger the better. I chose Swarthmore. Again, I have no idea why, except that its reputation had a combination of obscurity, perversity, excellence, radicalism, that seemed just right. Going to Harvard and Princeton, which were other choices, just seemed too conventional. I was into perversity—that struggle for individuality—and Swarthmore fit the image I had in my mind.

My expectations got blown so early at Swarthmore that I actually have lost track of what I expected. The experience of college was so different from my expectation that I simply lost track of any future. Whatever interests I thought were mine seemed to dissipate. In some ways I felt lucky to survive Swarthmore in body and mind.

Having believed I was special and brilliant, I discovered that I wasn't particularly special and I certainly wasn't brilliant relative

to the other highly motivated students around me. I was something
of a self-styled existentialist and tried to write a few philosophy
papers in my customary fashion. The members of the faculty
thought I was some kind of oddity. Although I did try to fit myself
into the mold, the rigors of the scientific method and textual criticism were absolutely not for my brain. I had the image of loafing
under an oak tree on the side of a hill, contemplating my navel
and coming up with fine thoughts, and that did not seem to be
what was going on at Swarthmore. I should have been in the library.
After two years of starting to major in philosophy, I took the looser
path and majored in history.

More important, a very desperate personal feeling came over
me. In high school I had established a scaffolding of security and
self-image. When the scaffolding was knocked out from under me,
my vision shortened until survival and a little bit of approval were
all that I was looking for. I assimilated the goals of Swarthmore,
which were to go on to graduate school in whatever I happened
to fall into as a major. Half the education came by accident. I
didn't quite find my scaffolding again. I spent four years, in fact,
without that sense of resting securely. I ended up feeling I was a
problematic sort of person, preoccupied with a combination of
general psychological problems and loneliness. I have damn little
to say about the rest of it.

What I needed was people more than education. Therefore I
joined that scruffy dirty group that was into cafe-style life, where
everything was conversation. I took my turn writing poems and
all the rest of it, but really for false reasons. I surely was not a
poet. Those poems formed my credentials for that particular radical, slightly off-center group that I always had a taste for. Among
them I could find what I wanted, the intensity of personal relationships.

Education was the institution's goal, however, and so I dutifully
proceeded to graduate school in American history at Harvard. That
certainly was not the finale I had expected when I entered Swarthmore, but at the finale I certainly had no idea of anything else to
do.

I quickly recognized that I was not suited for graduate school.
It offered the rarified intensity of a library experience, hours and
hours of reading books, when I was looking or feeling for another

kind of experience. I quickly developed mononucleosis. Something else would have happened, surely, to get me out. I had lasted six months.

In any case, when everybody I knew had managed to find a way to get out of the Army, I seemed to find a way to get into the Army. In June of 1961 I ended up going down as an enlisted man for basic training at Fort Dix, and had that experience which more than equaled every other shock I had had in my life. It was just insane there. Insofar as one learns in life that things are apt to be the very opposite of what we think they are, the Army was one of those lessons. It was opposite my expectations about the United States as a democracy, because obviously the military system is completely authoritarian. Totalitarian. The most logical, inefficient purpose of the Army is to obliterate individuality. Having had my individuality cultivated to a fine point up to that moment, that was quite an experience. I developed a lot of hatred toward authority in the Army, a lot of intense hatred. Probably the most extreme hatred I have ever felt. But at least the Army gave me a confidence that I could put up with almost anything, just by the fact that I had survived it.

I got out in December of 1961, went home to live with my parents, took up the writing idea again. My parents were extremely indulgent of me, financing sympathetically my attempts to find myself during this period. My father was general manager and vice-president of a shoe factory in Massachusetts for forty years or so, a good-paying job. My mother never worked from the time I was born, except in politics. She was sympathetic to the Left, he was sympathetic to the Right. Toward me they were certainly generous in the extreme. They were of the school which believed that little Junior has to find himself, and they continued to believe that through all my incredible permutations.

I developed a ritual. Every morning I went to the Boston Public Library, sat there writing or thinking until the end of the afternoon, and then went home. Eventually I completed one of the short stories. I probably had a few other obscure activities in this period. I did take up the violin. It seems a very lost time.

At some point I decided I had better find a job. Since I was a writer and interested in the arts, I thought I should work as cultural reviewer for a newspaper. So I assembled the names of ten newspapers around the country, wrote some wordy, pompous reviews, mimeographed them with a pompous letter, and sent them out to the editors of several papers. I received one positive response from the Providence *Journal.*

During the summer of 1963 I worked for the Sunday *Journal,* writing on concerts at Tanglewood and the Marlboro Music Festival, reviewing shows at the Museum of Modern Art. Again my parents were basically subsidizing me, because I would make a week's project out of one article for which the newspaper paid me twenty dollars. I was losing, not earning, money. But it was the first re-contact with the real world. I saw my name in print over articles, received generally favorable responses. I realized that I could review well. In the arts that I knew least about, particularly painting, I was able to review the best. It was something.

The entertainment editor felt I had a potential and wanted to hire me full time. He explained, however, that in the newspaper business one has to go through the basic apprenticeship as a reporter before one does a specialty like reviewing theater or music or movies. I accepted all that without flinching and thought it might be fun. They assigned me as regular reporter for the local news bureaus in small towns around Rhode Island. I was to cover the basic police, fire, school committee, town council, Mrs.-Smith-is-seventy-five-years-old, Mr.-and-Mrs.-Magoo-have-been-married-fifty-years (with pictures), human interest stories—the whole collection of local small-town reporting. I had no qualifications whatever. It was strictly on-the-job training.

To make it worse, they put me on a cycle of filling in for people on vacation, so I was never anywhere longer than two weeks. I would go to a town and have to understand it in a day, go out and cover a town council or school committee meeting without any idea of what the hell was going on. It was journalism's basic training. At the end you supposedly could go into any place and figure out the situation by means of purely professional skills, instincts, and questions, so long as you got the names straight. I found I never got beyond the level of trying to get the names straight.

They finally settled me in a very nice portion of southern Rhode Island where I did a minimal amount of work, played the violin during working hours with a local landscape painter who lived upstairs from the newspaper office, found a few good fishing streams nearby, and more or less suffered through the job without any typical newspaper aggression or frustration. I grew to enjoy covering the people in the towns; reporting on them was something else again. It was fun to sit down at school committees and town councils and to see local officials pushing and pulling the gears of local government. But as to making fools of them in print, that was not my instinct. I took very seriously what they were doing, more seriously than a good newspaperman should.

At a certain point it all came to a head. I had a chance to get the job as art critic because the current man fell sick. Then it turned into a big dispute between management and the union. I don't remember who won. In any case, I didn't get the job. I realized that I must stay around doing local news forever. My superiors, meanwhile, realized that my general reporting was not very good. They also caught me playing violin during work hours, playing duets with this crazy painter upstairs from the newspaper office. I think I quit just shortly before they fired me.

I stayed in Providence. I bought an old Bolex and started a little filming around the city. I shared an apartment with a friend who was writing a novel. Again I started taking money from my parents. Again I was thinking that one of these possibilities might work out, but I had no idea *how* it was going to work out, and that I was not even that active an agent in working it out. The individual accomplishments that I had done—the reviews, the little films—I saw as good, even exceptional. But in terms of relating them to the world, I had no idea how, and therefore I did not know how to feel, since again I was in the parasitic position of taking money from my parents. By this time I was twenty-three or twenty-four.

The film interest gradually possessed me. I was splicing little pieces of film that I had taken here, there, and elsewhere, making poetic images. Finally I regarded the work seriously enough that, after this mucking around, I returned to my parents' home and enrolled in television and film production courses at Boston University. I found my television production extremely exciting—a much richer use of the medium, in fact, than I have seen to this day. In film production I met Bob, who became a very good friend and formed a big part of the next years of my life. He was in it more seriously than I was, and I became his loyal friend and assistant.

When the courses ended I tried to get an internship at WGBH, the educational television station in Boston. That seemed to be a good way to get out of the house, get some money, get into a television career. WGBH rejected me. I was actually rather bitter about that, because my T.V. production was, as I say, still the best T.V. I have ever seen. But again it was a measure of something, which I do not understand, that one rejection was enough to make me say "fuck T.V." I don't know why. Obviously if I had really been this person wanting to do television I would have found another way to do it, there would not have been any problem.

So again I was doing nothing, except working with Bob, who was constantly making small films. I spent a lot of time with him, contributing to editorial work, camera work, and almost any other aspect you can name. Again, there was no money in any of it. But it was a very close relationship.

It finally occurred to me, in 1965 or 1966, that I had reached the bottom of the barrel. A neighbor of my parents, who owned a business importing scissors, had several times said to my father that he would always have an opportunity for me. Somehow, although I had never taken it seriously, the offer lay in the back of my memory. Now I reached back and grabbed it.

I finally moved out of my parents' house. I started learning the scissors-import business and selling to retail stores. I began to acquire something I had not had; not simply money, but a little basic dignity. In spite of all the indulgence that my parents had shown me, I still believed that you had to earn money at what you were doing.

I was very enamored of Harry, the man who owned and operated this business. As a child I had been close to him. Now he became someone I almost hero-worshipped. He was in his late fifties, early sixties. Throughout most of the day I sat opposite his desk watching him dictate letters, talk to customers on the telephone, issue orders. Showman that he was, he played delightedly to his audience. Harry became a real model for me. I worshiped his image of power, effectiveness, virtuosity, manipulation. I had never seen any one manipulate and move things around. He knew how to tell white lies, black lies, green lies. He knew how to phrase the same idea in different ways for different people. Here before my eyes was a whole set of skills that I had studied in college; history, after all, is made up of them. But I had completely missed the point. Here I sat across the desk from a man who was really shaping a situation.

During these same months I was involved with Bob. By way of a friend in the drama world, he brought me into contact with a small Boston theater and suddenly I was a director. I had never directed any plays, but now I directed several. What a mismatched trio we made: my two companions, talented but definitely down-and-outers; and I, a rising businessman and struggling theater man, whose romantic life was in a state of incompletion. My life was really two lives; scissors by day, theater after dark.

Because it was a small business, I got the hang of it quickly enough. I started to acquire titles: vice-president, etc., etc. I began to take myself a little bit seriously. On the other hand, I was still carrying guilt from my whole upbringing, my college experience, my arts involvement. I was embarrassed with friends who were in the academic world, the arts world or, by that time, friends who were seriously in the radical political world, for I was doing what I had once despised and my friends still despised. The bind of guilt hurt me, particularly because my friends in the New Left were extremely self-righteous and I was quite unsure of myself. How could I justify dealing with a company in Brazil that obviously was living off low-wage, somewhat exploited workers?

My first trip to Brazil, in 1969, affected me very deeply, agitated my system perhaps to its most extreme of my life. Those *favelas* terraced along the dusty hillsides of Rio de Janeiro, shack upon shack filled with the poorest people I had ever seen—they ripped the heart out of me. When I returned to the United States I felt a desire I had never quite felt that intensely: to be selfless, to give myself away to something bigger, to subject myself into service of the whole unbelievable, undefinable, unimaginable plight of all the people being screwed over in the world.

One day I went into the Harvard Cooperative Store at Harvard Square. They had those hard candies on the counter where cigarettes and postcards are sold. I lifted the basket off the counter and walked outside to the people waiting in line at the Harvard Trust Company next door. I went up and down the line giving out free candies. It does not seem related to the New Left or radicalism, but in my mind at that moment I believed I had to dispense some justice to those people in that line on a cold and windy winter's day. And I did it. A couple of days later, in fact, I went back to the Harvard Trust Company, walked upstairs to the office of one of their executives, and told him that I had been the one handing out candies. The incident is completely trivial and absurd, but somewhere within me it connected to a larger issue.

That same week I walked with a good friend past a Boston firehouse where the firemen were lounging out front—arm in arm I walked with a male friend of mine, in almost a homosexual posture. Was it my usual perverse instinct to provoke? Yes, but more than that. For a moment I wanted to expand my old perversity into a doctrine of virtue. In both these incidents I acted as I never had before and probably never will again, because I went into them with incredible conviction and amazing lack of fear. I thought I was going to be a saint.

For a few weeks I walked along the edge of something that seemed as if it might change my life completely, but I didn't take the decisive steps. The vision of extreme mental instability held me back. The psychiatrist whom I was seeing at that point actually considered putting me into an institution. For the preservation of my sanity, I let passivity take me over.

Gradually the guilt subsided and with it the desire for sainthood. Gradually I discovered that most of the condemnations of business that had filtered down to me, either in actuality or through my imagination, were so skewed as to be almost unbelievable. It was at this point that I began to take a positive angle on my varied experiences and began to feel that most of what one learns is so provincial and parochial, so biased and meaningless, based on so little real information, that any judgment of one world by someone in another world is likely to be nonsense.

Soon I gained my legs in the business situation. And sure enough, hero-worship began to transform itself into competition. Harry's total coverage of all aspects of business began to seem a little suffocating. I began to feel denied of territory that I thought should be mine. For the first time I was beginning to feel really self-confident and I wanted more credit, more money, more authority, some ownership. He owned and ran the business. Had I been assistant shipping clerk or had I been president, it would have made no difference. Harry used titles to serve his own purposes.

But he got distracted; his wife became ill and slowly died, an event which put him out of action for a year. During that period I started to run the business myself. When he returned and wanted his territory back, I was not in a mood to relinquish the ground I had won. I had not quite realized how much ground I had won.

For two years there were fights and lawyers and obsessions and anger and a tremendous amount of ugliness and, for me, a long experience with a psychiatrist as I tried to figure out what to do. I could not imagine myself really on my own, completely self-supporting, self-sufficient, doing what I wanted to do in my way. But I could not remain subservient, either. The psychiatrist experience—how does one recapitulate four or five years, twice a week, and one group session a week? I can't. All I can say is that it was what I needed more than anything else during this period of crisis. The basic question about me and my work was reaching a head.

During these same months I continued working with the film people. After a documentary on Joan Baez, I worked on one about returning Vietnam war veterans and another about heroin addicts. Here, too, a crisis developed. For six or seven years I had sustained an intense relationship with Bob, a relationship in which I was subordinate, but one which my ego needed to keep myself feeling that I still had a place in the art world. Bob and I disagreed about where to place the focus in the heroin addicts film. Usually I would have conceded, but now I didn't, and the disagreement became a quarrel and then a feud, until finally I ended the relationship. It was an ugly ending, ugly because we could not express or even understand what we were going through. I was fearful and sad to see that dependency end, but also relieved because I regained some freedom.

Meanwhile I met the woman I was to marry. With Elizabeth I enjoyed for the first time a satisfying relationship with a woman. There was a deep feeling of completion, a feeling that we belonged together. For the first time in my life there was somebody in my corner whom I trusted. Moreover, she was an excellent artist and that gave me another kind of completion.

1969, 1970, 1971—a lot of elements were coming together, a lot of issues were climaxing at the same time. I met Elizabeth, I broke up the friendship with Bob, and then I finally left Harry. Finally!

When it was all over, I began to see where I ended and the rest of the world began, what ground was legitimately mine to assert myself on and what ground was not legitimate, how much of what I was feeling was simply projection out of myself and how much was a feeling that I had a right to assert as much as anybody else had a right to assert anything. When I resigned the presidency of the scissors firm, I was finally making that assertion.

Elizabeth gave me a lot of support during these years. I did a lot of talking and she was there as a trustworthy listener, critic, partner. It was a dependency in which I did not lose strength, but gained. Gradually I believed that I could start my own business, finding some factory that I could represent in the United States. Late in 1972 I incorporated myself in the name of Lawrence Rubin Resources. I thought it was just a matter of taking a trip to Brazil, visiting some factories, and then setting out on the road toward my own business and some modest success.

Of course it turned out to be much more difficult than that. The first contacts I made were unproductive. Nothing worked out. In order to survive, Elizabeth and I had to start a real estate business. We hustled houses for two years, not very profitably. Finally, one of the Brazilian companies responded to my letters, invited me down to confer, and offered to pay me a retainer for my marketing strategy and product advice while they developed a position in the United States market. My wife and I immediately abandoned the real estate business that neither of us loved.

So here we are—she painting her canvases and teaching part time in a local community college; I operating Lawrence Rubin Resources. We have survived. More important, I enjoy my work and am satisfied by it. I am fortunate that I operate from the home. I can conduct most of the day's business in my pajamas, if that is my impulse. On the side I can enjoy my other pleasures. Turning on the radio I can perform my daily hour of saxophone (which has succeeded the violin) in harmony with John Coltrane or Weather Report. If it is a golden day at the right time of year, I am apt to go fishing or play golf. Since no one directly oversees me, I have the pleasure of doing my dress-up and my business negotiations at choice.

Being the one who is at home most of the time, I have quite a bit of domestic responsibility. My wife and I have struggled for years to reach a satisfactory balance. I certainly was brought up with the idea that the woman should do almost all the housework, while the man does the "real" work. My wife is a liberated woman and I'm only a partly liberated man. It has been somewhat of a struggle, because some chores—cleaning floors and toilets, most of all—do not come easily for me. I have had to learn a balance between my work responsibilities and my domestic responsibilities, and sometimes I resist the learning. Similarly, on certain days Elizabeth comes home and wants to tell her stories when I want to tell my stories first. It is not easy to find the balance between who is getting sympathy and who is asking for it, who is doing the work and who is expecting the work to be done, who is exercising responsibilities and who is taking them for granted. Almost every aspect of our home life seems flexible, changing from day to day, never fully settled. It is settled on an existential basis, as the situation evolves.

We have no children at this point. I would like children. Because of the insecurity in starting a business, we delayed the decision. Now that it becomes clear that I have no more security today than three or four years ago, and that in fact I will never have it, we decided to have children. Parenthood will be the biggest test of how our two careers can fit with family life.

As an individual entrepreneur, I am always on the edge of great success or great failure, at almost any time possibly made or possibly broken. That precariousness somewhat cramps my brain, though not my style. In order to sustain my business and life style, I must keep starting and building anew. At this point I need to develop relations with new factories so that I can reach a greater level of economic security. I know that I will have to go through that arduous experience of starting cold again, developing new factory contacts, new customers, the initial introduction of self, creation of one's credibility, all over again. That is a price I pay for my freedom.

But the price is also part of my satisfaction. I did not like the academic world because of the distance from the events you study. Business brings you close. You are in factories, you meet workers and management, you travel among people in diverse countries. You can make something happen that was not there before. Business combines the personal and the impersonal, a blend I never found in the art world or the academic world. The facts of business are price, quality, and delivery—objective facts. They remain, no matter how much one personally intervenes, but they shift and bend in response to one's intervention. It's a game. It's a weaving of the personal among those objective forces. That dynamic keeps me in contact *with* the world and alive *to* the world. There is no tenure in business. That constant stimulation, at times overstimulation, keeps me alive and excited.

As I said in the beginning, if something happened tomorrow to change my situation, I would not be surprised and would not hesitate to change with it. If Hollywood called me tomorrow, surely I would go. I don't think Hollywood will call me tomorrow, but if they did I would feel prepared to go. In fact, after all these experiences I feel prepared to go almost anywhere and do almost anything.

The obsession of my life has been a dependence on other people for definition of myself, a fear of authority, a fear of asserting myself. In response I have perhaps overasserted myself in order to overcome those feelings which seem to me the feelings of weakness and not the feelings of a man. Work is my form of overcoming my fear of my own weakness.

I think that work is essentially a therapy. Therapy and distraction and game. Whatever psychologists and anthropologists and sociologists would call it, it is something I need to make the game of life fun.

8
A Child of the Sixties Grown Up

by Arn Strasser

"The reader knows himself as he was twenty years ago and he has also in mind a vision of what he would be, some day. Oh, some day! But the thing he never knows and never dares to know is what he is at the exact moment that he is. And this moment is the only thing in which I am at all interested."

William Carlos Williams

There have been many false starts in the composition of this essay. This is by no means the first draft or the fourth. Just thinking of the 1960s is enough to get me entangled in a hundred subplots. The cast of characters seems endless, as I return to the crashing energy of those times. Now I must select out of this mélange a story, so that we can be reminded of what we have been through.

The fact that I can ask my ghosts and memories to leave, at least for a while, is simply an added, personal reason for getting down to a final draft at last.

Growing up

It is fitting that this essay be written from the vantage point of middle age, because in the Sixties we included middle age among our enemies. We had been taught that when we reached that phase of life and if we met the qualifications of being white, male, and middle class, than we would reach Respectability, Stability, Career, and Family. In other words, you did your job, you kept your mouth shut, and you received your due material reward. To us in our twenties, it seemed like a death sentence, just another reason for dropping out. We not only didn't trust anyone over thirty, as the maxim went, but shouted that no matter how old we got, we would never get old.

That is not how my story begins, though. I grew up in Great Neck, New York—white, male, and middle class. My father is Swiss and my mother English. They migrated to the United States in 1945 from Zurich, Switzerland, with four children. I was the second youngest, three years old at the time, and the only son. Neither of my parents ever changed jobs. My mother was a hard-working housewife. My father worked as a buyer and representative for a Swiss supermarket cooperative. Every morning he went off to the station, carrying his European briefcase, to board the Long Island Railroad, read the *New York Times*, and work until 5:30 in his office in the city.

We were a close-knit and stable family. Year after year we lived in the same three-story stucco house on that shaded suburban street. Sunday morning after Sunday morning we went to the community church, where I learned my moralistic liberal Protestantism. Sunday afternoons in summer we drove in our Nash down the narrow country roads to Sunken Meadow Beach, all six of us singing together.

It was not always peaceful. To this day my father accuses me of singing deliberately off key just to make him angry. And what an anger he had! He and I were often at loggerheads: about the mess in my room, where I had built a fantasy world of tiny cars and commercial enterprise; or about my peculiar dazed attitude in the midst of school work. I would hide behind my mother's skirt, a mother's boy, against my father's eruption of rage.

I was a shy boy, who played happily alone. I watched Captain Video on early T.V. and before that I listened to years of Jack Benny and the Hit Parade on radio. I wore a Davy Crockett hat, idolized Mickey Mantle, and rode a Schwinn bicycle with fat tires and a push-button battery-powered horn built into the crossbar. I don't remember growing up as being easy but I remember it never lacked love. I had the privilege of being in a family where the love between my parents and the love for the children and the love of the children for each other never wavered.

During my teens I began, proudly, to develop "unconventionalities." I recall my mother talking to a neighbor across the fence, pointing to me and affectionately saying, "Arnold, there, likes to listen to this 'rock and roll'." I read *Mad* magazine in its early phase. I listened late at night, with the radio under my pillow, to the ravings and wonderful stories of Jean Shepard. My sister Jeanette went off to Swarthmore College and brought back the black-sweatered intense intellectualism of what I suppose could be called collegiate beatnik. My sister Doreen spent the summer in the artists' colony at Provincetown, prompting my mother to wonder where she had failed when she searched the shanties for her wayward child. My sister Elizabeth and I waited in the background for our turn.

In 1961 I graduated from Great Neck High School, ready to be catapulted along with the rest of my class into the college boom of the Sixties. I was a conventional son who would follow in his father's footsteps. I would become a supermarket executive, using my father's connections and an education as a marketing major in a special program at Michigan State University.

Going midwest

My conventionality didn't last long. Almost as soon as I fell into the rah-rah Fifties atmosphere of MSU, my simmering rebelliousness asserted itself. That first semester I lived in a special dorm floor designated for marketing majors in what was to be an experiment in specialized education. We had a business "resident assistant" on the floor, Jack Lyons, who looked like a Harvard intellectual and wore baggy khakis, but whose stated single object in life was to make a million dollars. I always wondered whether he did.

The educational experiment broke down almost immediately. The young business majors were more interested in pranks and women than in business. And I soon discovered that I was less interested in business than in studying the liberal arts and curing society's ills. After a lackluster high school performance, I was determined to get good grades and prove my intellectuality. I was the guy everyone left studying on Saturday night. I also dressed as sloppily as possible and joined the daily gathering of campus artists and politicos who shared Spiro's coffee house with more collegiate elements. We spent hours looking artistic, discussing politics and culture, and smoking cigarettes. I first became a sociology major, then settled into political science. Only in my senior year, when I met Dr. Vernon Lidtke, did I become intensely interested in history.

Dr. Lidtke's lectures sparked my fascination with European history, especially the Weimar era in Germany and the rise of Hitler. He instilled in me a love of teaching and gave me a historical perspective that allowed for making judgments. History became a crowded stage, dominated more often than not by the egotistical, the greedy, or the simply insane. Constantly the working classes, the ordinary people, were fooled and sent to slaughter in wars perpetrated by economics and national chauvinism and petty jealousies. I found I had a love of this history that went behind the scenes and exposed the props behind what the traditional historians had described as historical Truth.

I began a process of intense questioning that was to last many years and that affected all aspects of my life. In academics, I questioned the encroaching behavioral approach to sociology, political science, and even history. C. Wright Mills became a hero, and my black-and-white Mills volumes were worn from reading. He combined a critique of American society with a high moral purpose and an unshakable belief in down-to-earth democracy, all of which provided the intellectual framework of the early New Left. And he drove a motorcycle to work; we didn't forget that. I also regularly read *I. F. Stone's Weekly* and for years that journalism jostled me into thinking.

At the same time, I questioned the customs I had grown up

with. I went out with women, but not exactly on dates. I had lovers and relationships, but never thought of marriage. I wore blue work shirts and holey sneakers, and grew a beard.

My parents joined thousands of others who were anguishing over the changes. Whatever expectations they had had for their son were disintegrating before their eyes. Their son had become a protestor and had to be dragged to the barbershop and said weird things and had no idea of future, career, or family. My father told me I had been duped by the Communists, my mother exploited every opportunity to keep me as undisheveled as she could. I came back from visits at home, during those four undergraduate years, bringing clean work shirts and leaving my parents bewildered.

In 1965 I graduated from Michigan State, a twenty-two-year-old Bachelor of Arts with honors in political science, who refused to stand for the pledge of allegiance to the American flag. And then? Whatever my parents believed, I *did* have an idea—or really, two ideas—for the future. In September I entered graduate school at MSU with the intention of becoming a historian. For the next two years I worked with Dr. Lidtke as his teaching assistant and enjoyed what was, despite the university's Gargantuan size, a personal intellectual atmosphere.

At the same time, I became more intensely involved in campus politics. Ten thousand miles away, the war in Vietnam escalated, and then in *Ramparts* we read of MSU's direct involvement—via the CIA and Wesley Fishel—in that war. Protest time had come. I helped set up the campus chapter of the Students for a Democratic Society, attending the first of what became, over the years, hundreds of meetings. A great tribal experiment was initiated with those meetings. The constant struggle was to communicate, to bring something productive out of what was often a chaos of egos (particularly, as we were later reminded by feminists, male egos), with perhaps a few government agents thrown in. We spent hours at the mimeo machine and on the picket lines protesting housing discrimination, the lack of student rights, and the war. To the participants' complete amazement, we occasionally had real results. This was in the renaissance period of SDS, the early days represented by the Port Huron Statement's ideals. I am still a believer in those romantic notions of participatory democracy and remain a critic of both state capitalism and state socialism.

Sometime in the fall of 1967 I saw a beautiful, mysterious woman

wearing a red scarf and studying Greek. I became instantly infatuated, then fell in love. By winter, Marian and I were living together.
We soon settled comfortably into a more or less traditional set
of male-female roles. I typed poetry and functioned alternately
as graduate student and protestor. Marian cooked the meals and
went to classes. We both had motorcycles, and I still remember
the familiar sight of her yellow slick raincoat and her yellow Suzuki
roaring off to her morning class. By the summer we were inseparable, in love, and "a couple." We drank wine and ate romantic
steak dinners, alone together.

In the spring of 1967 I graduated with a Master's degree and
accepted a full scholarship offer for a Ph.D. history program at
Brown University. When the summer ended, I tied my motorcycle
on the back of my Ford Falcon and headed east, while Marian
remained in East Lansing to finish her degree. I felt a sadness at
parting, but also an exhilaration at beginning a new phase of my
life. The country was in turmoil. Old institutions and values were
being shaken one by one. The questioning was becoming more
cataclysmic. LSD entered the scene, flower children inhabited
Haight-Ashbury, and the Beatles produced Sergeant Pepper. Antiwar protests multiplied as the Vietnam conflict escalated and Americans saw pictures of American napalm raining upon scurrying
Vietnamese peasants. I drove into Providence, Rhode Island, with
a feeling of anticipation, long hair blowing in the wind.

Going east

It was a city of contrast: the university on the hill, surrounded by
colonial brick houses and an air of smug elitism; and the drab
working-class districts, ruled by a corrupt mayor, the Mafioso, and
a reactionary police department, lying under the hill like a fiefdom.

I lived in an apartment overlooking Italian grocery stores and
restaurants. As I went to class, I passed through the smells of
dark Italian coffee and fresh baked bread of the outdoor markets.
I loved to walk across the Brown campus, where the prep school
atmosphere mixed with pockets of the counterculture. I mingled
with the political activists, the theater people performing avant-
garde participatory "be-ins," and the artists down the hill at the
School of Design.

The history department and I were always at odds. They wanted a career-minded historian; I wanted a relevant, activist study of history. More than that, as the latest news accounts from Vietnam increased my anger and frustration, I wanted to make history. By the winter I had made a name for myself as a campus radical spokesman (not spokesperson yet). I helped engineer a sit-down against a military recruiter, during which the cops dragged forty of us out of a building. I began daily contact with the campus chaplains and in particular with Rev. Dick Dannenfelser, who became a friend and counselor. The chaplains' office served as the buffer zone between the administration and the nonconformist elements of the student body. Protest at Brown was, and remained, primarily of the polite variety, neither side willing to go to extremes. The chaplains sat on the horns of their liberal dilemma, diffusing protest but also supporting it.

It was a year of protest, and also poetry. One evening I went to hear Denise Levertov and was so moved by her poems and her presence that I wrote her a poem of celebration. She had asked whether reading poems really meant anything in a time of war and turmoil. I wrote that her words were life and life was what we were fighting for. Toward the close of the evening she had mentioned William Carlos Williams, sparking my interest in his work. During the next few years, as I read everything Williams had written, I became influenced—in my own writing as well as in my living—by his clarity and by his emphasis on place, on the moment, and on the American idiom. Later, Allen Ginsberg, Gary Snyder, and Pablo Neruda also served as guides. There has always been a tension in my life between the desire to write poetry and to draw on the one side, and on the other side the need to earn a living and function in society. I have generally opted for the latter, but floating somewhere in my mind is the artist's dream of a studio.

The first year at Providence was exciting, surprising, and also confused. By the summer of 1968, however, my life seemed to come together. I dropped out of the history department, making official what already must have been obvious to all. Meanwhile Marian had finished her degree, so she and I were happily reunited. United but unemployed. With teaching jobs impossible to find, and with the national political scene heaving toward the Chicago Democratic Convention and who knew what tumult thereafter, we found ourselves contemplating a bold notion: Let's begin an underground newspaper!

I had done some drawings and an article for one of the original undergrounds, *The Paper*, which a friend had started in East Lansing. Now I asked Dick Dannenfelser whether the chaplains' office could provide seed money from its fund for "social action" projects. He was responsive, saying that two Brown students were thinking along the same lines and maybe we could connect. Soon we had a clear offer of three thousand dollars. The money really did germinate a seed and out of it grew the adventures of the next two years. We began preparations for the premiere issue of *Extra!*, a Providence, Rhode Island, underground.

It was almost literally underground, located below a church-sponsored coffee house in a basement office with a partly earth floor. Two Brown students, Doug Foskett and Dennis Sheehan, and Marian and myself, were joined by a loose group of other young people. Our first task was to build a wood floor under ourselves. And then came hours of meetings and frenzied sessions of writing, editing, and layout. We were proud of our first issue. On the cover was a fine photograph of a family on welfare. In the center was an article by Carl Oglesby, "An Open Letter to McCarthy Supporters," illustrated by a picture of three piglets cuddling together and by two scenes outside the Democratic Convention of 1968. One showed a Chicago cop (we said "pig" then) spraying Mace at a startled well-dressed crowd. The other showed National Guardsmen in gas masks patroling the downtown streets at night, eerily silhouetted against brightly lit skyscrapers.

Before long, the *Extra!* office had the look of a typical underground newspaper. Dusty stacks of unsold issues lay under the plywood layout table, a couple of old typewriters sat on a couple of beat-up desks, and pictures and posters were stuck upon every wall and door. The staff, along with visitors of every kind and sort, entered and left the office like characters in a drama with the pacing of a Marx Brothers film. We put the paper together in all-night layout sessions. We played the same six records over and over, Steve Miller's "Children of the Future" alternating with the Stones, Dylan, and the Beatles. To keep awake, we drank lots of coffee, ate fast food, and smoked cigarettes. Lengthy soul-searching discussions preceded every choice of word and illustration.

By the summer a core of people had developed who wanted to work on the paper full time. We became a collective entity vaguely titled "the Extra people": Marc, Fireball, Ramblin' Rose, Mary Jane, Dan, Marian, and myself. We found an apartment on the second floor of a tenement building in the working-class Italian neighborhood of Federal Hill. Around us we saw rows of identical wooden buildings, their gray paint peeling; and we smelled full cans of garbage; and we heard screaming family arguments, children being beaten, teenage hotrods roaring and Mafia Cadillacs purring down the street past parked cars, vandalized cars, and gutted cars.

Each morning we woke and made our schedules: to sell papers at various downtown corners; to deliver issues to distributors; to take care of office work; to do an interview. Each evening we reconvened to eat dinner together (a constant diet of brown rice goulash), to smoke grass, to talk, and to listen to music. We were constantly sitting in circles trying to decide, tribally, what we should do next in our work of creating the alternative society. We felt like examples of that society. Often we also felt like its warriors, engaged in a struggle not just for our own identities, but for the life culture against the death culture. Along with other Providence citizens, we read the daily headlines of bombings, trials, protests, and riots. But we also had tapped into the national communications network of the counterculture, and in each new packet of the Liberation News Service and each new issue of the San Francisco *Good Times* we felt in league with those who were confronting the government and corporations of America. Unmarked police cars shadowed us along the streets. Our phone was tapped. You could never quite trust a stranger who might be an agent.

We tried to change the nation, and also ourselves. One night we agreed to perform a church service at a progressive church, during which we symbolically burned bras and diplomas in the baptismal font, played David Peel songs, and danced for a new culture of joy, sharing, and change through self-criticism. We went to Woodstock, our red and purple truck creeping for endless hours along the New York Thruway until we managed somehow to enter Max Yasgur's farm and joined the half million celebrants.

When I think about this period, all the faces pass before me. I see myself in Mad Peck's studio-house, watching him draw a back page, fine minute tracings, with his cynical remarks hitting me like koans from a Zen master in a Cub Scout shirt. I see Marian and me lying on our oak bed. I see Marc wearing his infamous American flag headband around his head of long black hair. I see MJ laughing, running across a Newport beach. I see Ramblin' Rose with his eyes closed, rhythmically rocking to the indescribable energy of the MC-5. I see Fireball twisting his mustache as he answers the phone at the *Extra!* office.

By this time all of us were having bitter disagreements with our parents, based on differences both real and exaggerated. They had disowned us, now we disowned them. We accused them of complicity, of being blind, of having "sold out." We couldn't believe that they supported the war or, if not, that they wouldn't voice their opposition to it. We saw in our parents what the Port Huron Statement had pointed to in the nation: hypocrisy in religion, government, and business. They, in turn, thought we had gone bonkers. The clash was painful for both sides, but we bore the pain gladly, proudly, because it seemed a part of the breaking of all bonds of convention in order to stand in a free space.

Disagreements also took place among ourselves. I remember many arguments with Marian, followed by deep reconciliations of love. In these arguments I would turn moody, say "don't touch me" in order to have her say "I'm sorry" and to have her give the affection I craved. But of course such tactics made it harder for her to give affection. Sometimes we endured days or weeks of "being mad" and not talking to each other.

Arguments and silences likewise flared among the collective. Amid such volatility and intensity as we created, harmony would have been surprising. The disagreements were part of the process of personal and collective growth. In the spring of 1970, however, disagreement was not absorbed; it split us apart and ended the newspaper. The issue was violence versus nonviolence. This was the time of the Kent State killings, of intensified government repression, and of the Weathermen's bombings. The Movement was becoming contradictory, at once effective and self-destructive. Those same currents ran through us on the *Extra!* staff, sparking arguments, name calling, bitterness, righteousness, and finally dissolution.

Marian and I put out the last issue of *Extra!* on March 2, 1970.

Amid a two-page collage of pictures showing the symbols of our cultural revolution, a defiant little poem declared that the paper was breaking up, but not for lack of commitment.

Shortly afterward, I enacted that same defiance at a Kent State rally on the Brown campus. Wearing a black leather jacket, I went up to the stage, demanded a chance to speak, and then accused the assembled students of making meaningless gestures in an island of privilege. At the bottom of this hill, I told them, real people were working and facing the inequities of capitalism, while at Kent State four students had been shot, and in Vietnam countless peasant villages had been bombed. The students, predictably, booed loudly.

I had said my last words to Brown and, in fact, to Providence. It was also my last act as a Movement "heavy" and as a full-time organizer. I was exhausted. I stormed down from the campus and told Marian: "This is it. We're leaving."

For years we had been dreaming of California. The time had come, I decided. Only years later did Marian tell me that she had been ready to continue the paper in Providence. Such was our male-dominated relationship, however, that I never considered another decision than mine. I just took it for granted that Marian would come along.

Going west

Arriving in Berkeley was like landing on the shores of the promised land. Coming from the cold winters and gray afternoons of Providence, and from all that paranoia and negativity, we felt Berkeley to be nirvana. I picked ripe plums from the trees. I felt instantly at home amid the vibrant energy of Telegraph Ave.: the political posters; the freaks of every variety ambling down the street, many wearing red and yellow Vietnam pins; the natural food stores; the Whole Earth Catalog store; the ideas and collectives springing up everywhere. We sighed gratefully and found our place.

On a Berkeley hillside just up from the University of California, we shared an apartment with five other folks and lots of house guests. There was Audrey, a wise fourteen-year-old, and her boyfriend Rick, who was once her teacher. There was Joey, a writer, who studied Russian, played old folk guitar, and was something of a born-again Christian. There was Sue, a quiet UC student, and David, a quiet college dropout looking for a job, who eventually got together as a couple. Downstairs were a group of UC students who lived for mountain climbing and guitars; also Gary, who was writing a book on the New Physics; and Fred, an electrical engineer. Across the way was Ann, a teacher, who was looking for a place in the country. Across the street was Isobelle and another whole house of assorted folk.

But I was no longer a collective entity. In the summer of 1970 I was twenty-seven and entering another phase of my life, an introverted phase, a time of questioning my past and searching for new directions. I faced myself. Marian made a beautiful red shoulder bag, and in it I kept my black journal. I would sit in the Mediterranean Cafe and write poetry or record the details taking place on Telegraph Ave. Although Marian and I were in love and very much a couple, I was floating alone and trying to find a place to land. Not entirely alone—Bob Wolfson became a friend and compatriot and confidant, as did Andy and other men. In response to the feminists' challenge that men find emotional support elsewhere than from girlfriends and wives, I was beginning to do just that.

Meanwhile, Marian and I survived on various jobs. We sold the two Berkeley underground papers, cooked in a restaurant, painted the inside of an old office building, and finally worked at Berkeley's Ma Revolution food store.

It was a healing time. We experimented with macrobiotics, and I did yoga at an ashram. In my journal I wrote about "Zen Revolution," declaring that change must include both a political and a spiritual side. The spiritualists ignored Vietnam, poverty, and racism; the politicos abused their bodies and their personal relationships. I wanted to combine the impersonal with the personal aspects. I now thought not only of war and capitalism, but of food and ecology and my individual sanity.

Marian and I had been talking of having a child and in that first Berkeley winter, while making beautiful love, we conceived. On September 11th our daughter was born. I drew a big heart in my journal and wrote:

Baby born! In life wonderful contraction while all earth spinning and all subtle and glorious changes in motion. Near 6 A.M. first sticks her furry top of head, then whole head, then slow squeeze of whole body, so clean. I am awestruck and laid low by this consciousness expanding drug of natural childbirth. Muttering

power to the kids, but just beyond words. New Life Beginning.
And in my uni-verse new shift, new phase. Someone. And all
the world in different contour and all voices new and strange
and new delight of beginning.

We named our daughter Dharma Celia Sun-Ra. She filled my life
with an abundance of new love. Soon after the joy of Dharma,
however, would come the curse of Michael.

Whatever individual changes I was going through, the war was
continuing. The war became a nightmare, a bloody nightmare,
and we felt the pain of our humanity being burned and bombed,
we heard the screams of death. In response, Marian and I joined
the newly formed New American Movement, whose goal was to
establish a "humanistic, democratic socialism." The familiar meetings began—the parliamentary maneuverings, the long, heated discussions of position papers and right tactics and right strategies.
Reality split into two: the reality at NAM meetings and the reality
just outside the door. You had your NAM life and you had your
personal life, and neither sustained the other. After a few months,
I left NAM with a great sigh of relief.

It was in NAM that we met Michael. He had helped to conceive
the principles of the organization. He was brash, smart, and obnoxious. He was always making important phone calls. To Michael,
the smarter you were, the better you were, and the more worthwhile
your ideas, especially if they more or less agreed with his. The
intellectual would lead the working class, purely in an advisory
role of course, to its historical destiny where economic and social
justice would finally reign. Within the first few meetings, I disliked
Michael. I saw in him all the male qualities I was trying to eliminate
in myself. I was back in the school yard, feeling that terrible com-
petitiveness I hated so much. But that was not the worst part.

The worst was that Marian became infatuated with Michael and
they began to have an overt affair. It was to be simply that: an
affair. The intention was that Michael would stay with his wife
and Marian would stay with me.

But for me it was not simple at all. My jealousy erupted volcanically. I thought of nothing else but Marian and Michael together.
In pain I turned to Marian. I could not believe she was doing
this. I cried openly. She just looked at me coldly, without sympathy.
It was her way of breaking out of "the couple." It was also her

way of saying that I could not depend on her to prop me up or put me together. For years she had performed those services, she reminded me, along with the cooking and other traditional female work. But no more. She had enough, she said bluntly, of male chauvinism. After one particularly bitter argument, I moved out of the house on the hill. I drove off on my ten-speed bike for my own apartment. "Arn and Marian" had ended.

I felt a deep pain and sadness, as well as an enormous sense of loss. With these feelings, however, mixed an unexpected feeling of gain. Marian's feminism was her gift to me. It was a key to freedom—not freedom from her, but freedom for me. To be a liberated male—or more accurately, to be struggling to be liberated—to be willing to question the male prerogative, to share equally in housework and child raising, to be able to cry, to coddle, to mother, to be noncompetitive, to be gentle: these are qualities I will always strive for.

Coming full circle

During this troubled period I became fascinated with the writings of Wilhelm Reich. The more I read, the more guidance I found. According to Reich, the prescription for mental and physical health consists of three words: Work, Love, and Knowledge. To Work is to find a commitment and a joy in construction, to find one's calling. To Love is to release tension in the body, to give, to unite, to work off "orgastic" primary energy. To Know means to struggle for honesty and clarity and freedom. I soon adopted these three concepts as my goals and, during the past five years, have begun to reach them.

For my work I have chosen chiropractic—or perhaps it chose me. One day, in the midst of an unusually throbbing headache, I made an appointment with Dr. Elizabeth Moyer, a chiropractor whom a friend had recommended. I was amazed to find a doctor who used her hands to make the adjustment that brought a sudden sighing relief and who took the time to talk about diet and give me a much-needed colonic. A few months later, Marian and I took part in a pilot program of health maintenance. Each week our group of ten people would begin with a Tai Chi lesson, go in for a chiropractic adjustment, and then eat a nutritionally designed meal. The experience was so wonderful and instructive that it prompted

Marian to make a big decision; she would become a chiropractic physician.

After having been accepted at Western States Chiropractic College (and having ended the affair with Michael), she went with me and Dharma to live in Portland, Oregon. While Marian attended school, I took care of Dharma, gave my last effort to the splintering antiwar movement, and found a job delivering newspapers from my car every day at three A.M. That job must have been the gods' punishment for some ancient misdeed. In any case, it propelled me to the decision that I must—absolutely must—find that "Work" part of Reich's triangle. Trusting my instincts, in addition to some hard thinking, I applied to Western States and began my career as a chiropractic physician. I chose a work that I believed in, one that runs counter to traditional ideas of medicine and to the billion dollar drug industry. I chose a work in which I can be relatively independent; working in a corporation would, I knew, drive me mad. I chose a work that puts me in touch with people, who have always been my primary interest.

Work, and also Love. I met Karen and felt the rejuvenation of an openly romantic affair. Marian and I developed a friendly and trusting accommodation, living a few blocks away from each other, sharing equally the care of Dharma. At the same time I began communicating with my parents again. We relieved ourselves of the burdens of our conflicts. We created a space of mutual respect and let the differences remain, for the most part, untouched and unspoken. I rejoined the family and in a larger sense rejoined the culture. I talked to people, not about politics, but about more personal, concrete problems and more mundane matters. I accepted people's habits and weaknesses, avoiding righteous judgments while still objecting to social injustices. I accepted myself. Perhaps that acceptance is part of Knowledge.

The story of the past six years is too close for the telling. In four intense years of chiropractic college, I thought of little else but the human body and its health. Here, trying to fashion a practical counterweight to my political idealism and artistic visions, I changed as much as in the years in Berkeley. Now I am married to Diane and we excitedly await another child. We live in a small house a few blocks from the clinic. Dharma has lived here for six months and then will live for six months with Marian, who is spending the year in Europe. I am engrossed in the joy of being a chiropractor and a holistic family physician and in the frustrations of being an entrepreneur. Today I talked to a friend about sharing a studio where I might sneak away on my off hours.

I, like my parents, have a career and a marriage and children. As a child of the sixties, I am about to enter the eighties. I enter deeply affected by my past, still on the side of the life culture, against dictatorships, nuclear power, corporate farming, and the persistent ills wearing on the planet, but more realistic in a new time, more willing to compromise, more aware of personal needs. The 1970s has pretty much worn out what were once meaningful phrases but still I say it: I want to live in the moment, open to changes, challenging myself to remain truly alive. It's good to look back, to see what I can learn, but now I want to be again in that moment, in that new beginning.

9
Why in God's Name Don't I Have a Job?

by Steve Turner

A woman I went out with for a while in college once confided that her mother called me a "professional proletarian."

That revelation—part of some sort of emotional sparring match at the time (1955), I think—embedded itself in my memory word for word. The term was new to me, and I wasn't really sure it had to be considered entirely derogatory: the sound of "proletarian" in those Eisenhower-McCarthy days had a kind of dangerous swagger to it. But mainly I recall being as much pleased to learn that the mother talked about me when I wasn't there as I was piqued that she used sarcasm when she did.

148

It helped, of course, to know that it was fond sarcasm. We were on good terms, the mother and I, even though we argued about the ways of the world. In fact, I estimated that her disparagement was basically defensive—that she was reacting guiltily to my militant criticism of things called "status quo" and "conformity" (very hot stuff) by sticking pins in some of the other entries on my list of social criticisms.

That disparaging response of my own, however, has long since been replaced by a kind of vexed admiration for the woman's prescience. As it happened, she had her finger on what was to become a leading contradiction of my subsequent working life (dominant center, for the most part of *all* aspects of my life): the nonsynchronous combination of proletarian politics with a series of professional occupations.

At the time she labeled me, of course, I hardly knew professional *or* proletarian from a hole in the ground. I was a product of a small, calm, all-white Maryland suburb of Washington, D.C. My father was an administrator in the Foreign Aid program (after many years' service in another government department). My mother was a part-time editor. I had an older brother, younger sister, and friends. The upgrade of our family's modest affluence had led to my New England college, and beyond that was sure to bring me to one or more respectable stations in life.

I considered myself sided with society's underdogs—whom I discussed in absentia in comfortable living rooms and well-funded schools—but I was a romantic on the subject, grossly ill-informed. My views evolved not from personal experience, but from emotional response to pictures and tales of the Great Depression; from my parents' enthusiasm for the New Deal and Roosevelt; and from a deep source of captivated admiration for the works and characters of John Steinbeck.

Later I was to have jobs—in canneries, Army service, on a wheat ranch, and in a variety of social agencies—that brought me into sustained contact with wage workers, welfare recipients, black people. But at that time I knew poverty only as sung by Woody Guthrie, and the world of labor as illustrated by Thomas Hart Benton. My sheltered sentiments imputed nobility (and humility) to toil and toilers. I believed in reform government as the true revealed mechanism for expression of workers' and farmers' aspirations for happiness. Nay, I even saw government officials as saviors—remember the white-clad migrant camp manager in the film *Grapes of Wrath*?—and believed them the recipients of gratitude and love from the humble folk they helped.

I expected to be one of those loved and respected officials, of course, or something similar and clean. I never imagined a career in noble toil for myself. And I was ignorant enough not to know that my occupational inertia—bound for the necktie-clad professions—would carry me a great social distance from the factory gate, to a realm where people generally viewed noble toil and its practitioners with condescension.

But my girlfriend's mother did know that. As she foresaw, I never left the social track I had been started on, and in fact I attained several sorts of professional identities in my progress. But I also never split away from my ideological attachments. Instead, increased knowledge only clarified and strengthened the political-analytical bent on which I had begun in such an innocent and fuzzy way, and I moved steadily to the left as the years passed.

Did La Mama foresee that too? For the sake of her remembered wisdom, I hope she did. But if she did, why didn't she talk to *me* about it instead of her daughter? Why didn't she tell me more about life instead of leaving me to reap so much tension and error, and to find satisfactions so often under the shadow of concurrent frustration?

One thing never in question as I grew up was the need to work when adulthood was achieved. It wasn't simply the lack of inherited wealth around the house. It was that my father worked, my mother worked (after my brother, sister, and I completed the earlier stages of growing), and my friends' fathers and some mothers worked. In fact, they worked most of the time; activities at home with them were all after work. Weekends were sandwiched (often with considerable compression) between their work weeks.

More important, they obviously found their work significant. They dressed up for it, rose early to prepare for it, went off impressively in cars and trains to do it, and talked about it to each other afterward. Girls in my town had the mixed message of stay-home mothers and working mothers to untangle. But for the boys there was no confusion; work and manhood were unseparable.

Mostly, of course, that meant that manhood was inseparable from wearing ties and going to an office, but there was some variety. Neighbors included a barber and one of the fabled "men working in trees," as well as a research chemist and a school principal. Elsewhere in town lived a radio repair person and a welder. But most everybody else who worked went in to Washington to the government.

My own first work experiences, however, were very much proletarian. Between the end of high school and the end of college (at which point I turned into an Army lieutenant and became properly affixed in my social stratification), I did road construction, mail delivery, fruit picking, truck driving, and production line work in a cannery.

Each of these jobs came between sessions of the continuing educational process then defined as my natural and obligatory occupation. So each presented itself as a kind of side trip into a world I perceived as more robust, more elemental in its realities and relationships than either my student existence or the future of work it was likely to lead to.

Needless to say, the work experiences tempered that perception, stripping away successive layers of the romantic ignorance which burdened my views on wage labor. But the information and impressions acquired in exchange for lost innocence were important, and far from disappointing; these early excursions into payroll territory helped to confirm my political directions. And memories from these early jobs are now more vital in my mind than any recollections of much of the professional involvements which followed.

There was working on the highway, for instance. It was right outside Washington, at a time when the onset of Eisenhower, Nixon, McCarthy, and others had taken away my illusions about the top-to-bottom goodness of government; desires for employment in the domestic bureaucracy had been slammed away by the crude Republican performance (even though lower levels of government remained relatively unsullied, the purposes of such employment in the overall sense had been smirched). Complementarily, my father had transferred to the foreign aid administration, and my family had moved to Iraq. I had stayed behind with a friend's family to finish my last year of high school, and I took the road-building job to help earn my keep for the summer months.

The construction company was from Georgia, and when I applied I was warned by the foreman that the only job available was "nigger work": keeping the dry cement moving out of the main storage hopper, through the auger lifts to the batching towers which loaded the concrete-mix trucks. (Dry cement is very dusty, bad for the lungs, heavy to work with, and tends to pack on itself as it sits.)

With proud contempt for his easy racism, I said I didn't mind what kind of work I did. I doubt that I actually communicated my contempt—that is, I got the job. All the other workers around the batching plant were in fact black. Lord knows what kind of impression I actually made—in addition to being the white holder of a designated "nigger" job, I was a determined egalitarian of the "you're as good as I am variety." But we all got along well enough on the job.

I was stationed out in the sun, to poke and stir the cement. Periodically a local good old boy named Curly arrived in his ten-wheel dump truck to refill my big metal bin. In between deliveries, I did my steady best to get it all out through the grates at the bottom where the auger turned. (I never could get it completely emptied, but what other goal was there?) In addition to prodding the inert silt with the long poles, I had to beat the sides of the hopper with a big rubber hammer. I wore a filter mask for breathing, goggles for my eyes—badges of labor identity which rode (respectively) under my chin and atop my head when I was not pushing the cement. The dust covered me, setting up in decorative gray lines wherever my sweat ran most freely.

We were turning a three-lane road into four lanes, divided. So we truly ruined the rush-hour flow that used the old road. And one afternoon this brought me my first real exposure to symbolism in everyday life—in a brief drama of class, caste, and work identity entitled "The Turtle Which Did Not Piss on My Hand."

I was prodding away at the cement, not much left in the hopper. Traffic was so tied up on the road that Curly was late with his delivery. But the returning concrete batch trucks were being delayed too, so after a while I could rest; the tower was full, and they shut off the auger.

Then out came the turtle—tortoise, to be accurate, a regular garden box turtle. It crawled around the corner of the hopper, as covered as I was with cement dust. It was headed for the highway.

I tried to divert it. No good: it kept heading for the car wheels. And even though the cars were mostly not moving, it was clear that the turtle was dooming itself.

So I picked it up and headed across the road. The stalled cars were full of damp, hot, dressed-up, frustrated, government workers. I edged through them, totally messy, caparisoned with my eye and lung protectors, aware of my tanned skin and work-expanded muscles, grinning as I showed them the turtle which was getting where it wanted to be faster than they, the agent of its delivery being in their case the agent of delay. They stared through their windshields at me with distaste and apathy. I was happier to be on my side of the tableau than theirs. And the turtle, pleased somehow in its own dull, cosmic way, refrained from the urinary release tactic common to its kind when in a state of panic.

Picking strawberries in the Pacific Northwest, I came flashingly in touch with what work means when it is directly tied to each day's food and shelter. Predictably, the wages for picking were strictly piecerate: the more quarts you picked, the more you were paid.

I chose my lane in the vast field, and set off between the two rows of plants. It was hard to figure out whether crawling or stooping was the most efficient approach; neither was comfortable. Groveling along, I mindlessly picked berries as I came to them from plants on either side.

Coming up from behind in the lane next to me was a boy ten years old or so, one of several children accompanying a mother and father into the field (they had arrived, packed together, in an old, out-of-state car). He was much more adept than I. As he pulled abreast, he noticed that I was taking strawberries off from all around the plants between us. As I was now to discover, only the berries on my side of the plants were "mine" to pick.

"Hey," he said, and faster than I could have imagined, he had a pocket knife out and opened, pointed at me. His shoulder height was about at my solar plexus, but he was managing to look dangerous anyway. "Keep your goddamn hands off my berries," he said.

I gawked. He stared, still menacing me with the knife.

"Sure," I said. "Take it easy."

He put up the knife and went back to picking.

In the cannery, I stacked the full cases of peas as they came down the conveyor from the labeling-boxing machine. I worked with a crew of three others: my college roommate; a dramatically macho Oklahoman with a duck's-ass haircut; and a slight man in his mid-fifties named Haskell, who wore glasses and hummed or sang (falsetto) snatches of hymns when the line was running full speed.

We worked twelve-hour night shifts, ending about 5:30 A.M., stacking an average of twenty tons apiece per shift, working the whole time in the aroma of cooking peas and the clatter of the equipment (both of which were more oppressive further back along the production line). But coming out after shift's end into the late dawn—with the air fresh, bright, and cool—was a sensual experience hard to match. The body ached, but ached in the way that promises to end with sleep. The scummy throat and nose could be hawked and blown clean, and the incoming air was like water. The overall feeling was of health and competence, strength, pride in passing a test of work each night that brought me near the physical limit.

But it was my first experience with being driven near that limit by machines. In part, the satisfaction that made each morning so sweet was of having outdone the machines again, of having bested the factory and its line, and of having done so as part of a team of workers. The cannery equipment fascinated me, but the harder we had to work, the more that fascination dulled. The machinery took on an impassive and indifferent character, even slightly hostile; something that waited at the start of each shift to administer the test again. So even though I was enjoying the experience (and I had not tried to think whether I would want to be doing such work at Haskell's age, nor even whether I would like to attempt it year round—let alone whether I could steadily find such jobs), I joined the other workers in praising and congratulating the anonymous fellow employee who threw the pinch bar across the ears of the cannery transformer. It was a piece of sabotage perfectly timed to keep us in place several hours without working while repairs were made; had they dismissed us, all the fresh peas loaded in for processing that night would have gone to waste.

At that time, I had not yet separated management from machinery as the causal force that was actually assaulted by the pinch bar. But I understood that we were getting something of our own back, sitting on the dark loading dock just smoking and talking and resting as our wages amassed for free.

In the wheat harvest, the relationship with machinery and work was totally different. We got up with the sun, ate what would have been a big dinner at any other time of day, and then rode truckback to the cutting field. Other machines waited there; additional trucks, the big combines and their caterpillar tractors, the trap wagon with its barrels of oil and grease.

In the outdoor quiet of each fresh morning, we fired up those engines—one worker to each machine—and the diesel exhausts of the tractors put narrow gray columns straight up into the sky. Then we scattered over the rolling face of the field to get in the grain. The machines were direct extensions and expansions of each of our individual competencies. They gave us power and mobility, and their capacities actually made the harvest. We worked in concert with the machines, and liked and respected them.

I also liked the wheat land. It was magnificent in the visual sense, golden to gray-brown depending on whether the wheat was cut or not, rolling like flesh under skin, attracting the sexual and hunger responses at the same time. It was extremely dry and hot; two years' rain was needed there to grow one crop of wheat. The surface of the soil was a mulch of fine dust which powdered to a depth of several inches under the wheels of the trucks. The ranch, reputed to exceed 30,000 acres, went on and on before the eye, the sweeping undulation of it interrupted only by a line or two of telephone poles, and—if you were on a hill high enough to see it—the windbreak trees, the sheds and outbuildings and old windmill tower of the ranchhouse compound.

I drove a truck, as did my college roommate and one other worker. We chased the combines, roving around with dust clouds pouring out behind the tires, dust and chaff coating us in the cabs. We would meet the combines and unload them, and when filled, haul the grain five miles to the elevator at the railroad.

On afternoon runs, I used to stop at the tiny store adjacent to the elevator, and get four bottles of beer—two for me, two for my roommate. I had the first as I cleared the town and headed up the long hill back to the fields. It took the dust down, chilled the throat. It was the best beer I expect ever to drink, even though it was only three-point-two.

In my working life, this of all jobs most fully combined aesthetic and sensual pleasures, physical test and productive purpose. It paid $15 per day plus board and room (a cot in the bunkhouse), and for the brief time that I did it I loved it.

But the same work clearly brought its dissatisfactions to those connected with it year round, particularly the women so grimly isolated in residence at the ranch compound (the next nearest ranch was five miles away, and the nearest town of size was fifteen miles off). The boss's wife, for instance, often screamed out the door after him as he drove off to drink in town. She usually called him "You big fat tub of shit." Over in the crummy small house allotted to the foreman, there lived also his bitter and acrid wife (whose upper front teeth were missing) and her taciturn mother. The wife cooked for the crew, and appeared to hate every minute of it. One of the tractor drivers, a young and (to me) likable smartass named Ross, tormented her by sneaking a succession of cutting tools into the dining room—saws, files, etc.—with which, ostensibly, to cut the powerful crust on the pies she made for every meal. She finally went into a great rage and chased him out of the house with a broom (I had never seen this done before), then broke down in tears and was led to the bedroom by her mother. Ross was fired, and went on to some other tractor at some other ranch. She stayed where she was.

I returned, in the fall, to college. It was the start of my junior year, and the end of my excursions into wage work. These ventures across the social and occupational strata cumulatively had given me ammunition and assurance in the arguments I made for liberal social policies (most of my classmates seemed to be political conservatives). But that was as far as it went for the time being. The nonproletarian future was looming up in military form; I was about to enter the long eddy of the soldier period in my life.

Like many others at my college, I was supplementing my parents' financial support by taking a monthly stipend from the Reserve Officers' Training Corps (ROTC) program, run by the Army in this instance. In exchange for the money, we all took some courses in Military Science and Tactics (snore, snore), and once a week put on old-style soldier suits and did mindless drill and ceremonies on the football field. We also committed ourselves to two years' active service on graduation, and we received our commissions as 2nd Lieutenants right along with our diplomas.

With Vietnam yet to come, and the true story of Korea obscured by the infamous domestic/international Red Scare, the late 1950s were still a time in history when being in "The Military" was generally looked on as just another occupation—a professional occupation if one was an officer. With no wars in progress, moreover, the Army seemed to offer (and in fact did offer) a way to continue the relaxedly unfocused style of student life. In both college and military settings, one carried out assigned activities to satisfy institutional requirements established by someone else, long ago, and if those requirements were properly satisfied, rewards followed— grades and advancement in college, pay and promotions in the Army. It was not necessary, and in many ways not possible, to calculate whether endeavors in either school or Army had any significant connection with the larger reality of social intercourse and progress outside the institutional bounds. Institutional identifications, moreover, provided ready-made substitutes for serious reckoning about what life might be, could be, should be. Saying "I am a junior in college" provided both explanation and justification of existence. And although the terms of reference were different, "I am a lieutenant in the Army" did the same thing for me and many others. We never considered the Army a final destination; it was merely the next two-year interval in our metamorphosis. Who knew what would come next?

For me, that interval stretched to five years. I was trained in the game-like procedures of Communications Intelligence (COMINT: intercept their radio traffic and learn their secrets) and Communications Security (COMSEC: keep our secrets safe from them). I was sent to places all over the world. It was a period of travel, of experiences I probably couldn't have had any other way (I remind myself). It was also a time of basic change in personal situation; I got married, a condition I still share with the same partner, Anne.

And as it turned out, five years was the length of time necessary for my occupational desires to emerge clearly and concentrate sufficiently to start me in a new direction. I went into the Army with a vague intent to go on—sometime—into the diplomatic or consular service, or foreign aid. I even furthered that intent, albeit loosely, by requesting a one-year assignment to the Army Language School to learn Chinese (for which I traded an additional one-year commitment of time in uniform).

The pull from the direction of foreign service, however, was residual, not compelling. It was made up chiefly of father-followership plus the fading vestiges of youthful orientation toward government work. Domestic civil service potentials had been warped away long since, but might not the country's role in foreign assistance still be uncontaminated? Charitable? That hope evaporated in Korea, where, at the end of my second year in uniform, I finally joined the working Army in the field. It was a country strapped down and covered by the military presence. Although it reportedly had the largest civilian United States Operations Mission (coordinating all nonmilitary programs in the country, which of course includes police) in the world at the time, the effects of civilian aid were invisible. Among other things, despite the multibillions of U.S. dollars run through that Mission, not enough had been in the right channels to eliminate a national affliction called "The Spring Hunger," the period of wretchedness still visited on large numbers of rural Koreans as their winter stores ran out before the early new crops were ready for harvest.

That fact joined itself inexorably to an anecdote told me by my father after visiting Korea for an Asian regional economic development conference. He was informed by a Korean industrialist—hosting a lavish party for the conferees—that U.S. support had enabled Synghman Rhee's government and friends to smash the South Korean labor movement sufficiently that it was not expected to even start recovering for at least twenty years.

So I abandoned my ideas about foreign service work. But no definite alternative revealed itself. Like one of those magnetized needle-in-cork kiddie compasses, I changed direction only slowly, listlessly, uncertainly, toward a final alignment with my ideological underpinnings. True North, when reached, turned out to be a desire to work to *change* society's injustices and inequities, rather than simply discuss them as theretofore I had done.

It was a logical outcome, given my political inclinations. But my adjustment to the drift of the times and my life was so thorough that (I admit with embarrassment) it was not my own analysis that sparked the process of personal change and decision. It was the social upheaval of the Civil Rights Movement, breaking through the institutional cocoon I had wrapped around myself, that finally opened up my mind. Nor was the effect instantaneously full blown. Development of my new consciousness of social needs and work potentials began slowly when I became responsible for smoothing out racial conflicts among troops at the unit I was assigned to in Korea (I had the absurd duty of "morale officer," among other things); the draftees and one-hitch enlistees there particularly brought along the problems of the home society fresh and intact. News of protest activity in the States opened a vacuum behind my own cautious responses, and mocked my wish to avoid personal involvement in the strife. But it wasn't until two years later that my disaffection with official responses to the "race problem" was strong enough to push me irretrievably onto the new path. Symbolically that point came when I took annual leave (I was then on assignment to the National Security Agency) to do volunteer work at the landmark 1963 civil rights March on Washington. And even then, it took an early brush with the Vietnam War some months later to make the final break in my inertial attachment to the Army.

That was in the first part of 1964. I held the rank of Captain. Colleagues with my sort of experience in the Intelligence and Security Branch were beginning to get secret, plainclothes "advisor" assignments to Vietnam. I opted out. My resignation was approved in the summer, and in August Anne and I moved to Philadelphia—not for that city's sake, but because I had been accepted for graduate studies at the University of Pennsylvania. In keeping with my past pattern of status and personal development, my chosen approach to the new occupational future was through the acquisition of a professional degree in "Intergroup Relations."

By that time, Anne and I had been married four years. None of them were easy years. None—by far—had come near matching the pleasures of our courtship in the Monterey Peninsula area of California, where I was at the Language School and Anne was a college freshman. During the long summer, she shared a house with a roommate in Carmel while she worked as a waitress by day and, at night, performed as an actress in a local theater. She was nineteen, I was twenty-two. We did a lot of walking on the beach and going to coffee houses. (She had folksinger friends. It was a time when military people and folksingers still could mingle, although a friend of mine in uniform on his way to a club in Greenwich Village was chased down the street by an old woman who screamed "Warmonger, Warmonger!")

We were both on unfamiliar and liberating turf. She came from a suburb of San Francisco, not too far away, but was for the first time living on her own away from home. As for me, I was removed from all previous friends and acquaintances by 3,000 miles, in a geographical wonderland where it never snowed, where whales and seals swam in the Bay, where many of Steinbeck's scenes had occurred or had been imagined by the man himself when he lived there.

So we were both vulnerable to fascination; found it easy to find, in fact. Moreover, we meshed with each other in a crucial way: both of us displayed assurance and initiative, but it was not solid stuff in either case. Both of us needed the constant reaffirmation of a supporting soul in attendance.

That is a need which presents the supportive soul with a powerful weapon, of course—a fact which only manifested itself further on in the relationship. Given time apart, both of us might have outgrown some of the anxieties of that need. When orders came in midsummer posting me to Korea after December graduation, we probably should have started to aim for separation. But it was too late. We got married instead, despite the fact that I would not be allowed to have "dependents" with me at my station in Korea.

So we had four months of organized cohabitation, and then split. As it happened, Anne went to Asia and she left first; her father was a steamship company executive, and had obtained a discount fare ticket for her to travel to stay with *my* parents, stationed in Bangkok by then (still in the foreign aid program). My unaccompanied tour of Korean duty was to be only thirteen months long, so we thought of ourselves basically as one-year yo-yos, set to snap back to a stateside life together the following winter.

But complications set in, including (1) erection of the Berlin Wall, which caused extensions of all tours everywhere by three months, (2) Anne's consequent decision to come to Korea and "live on the economy" in Seoul, where we saw each other infrequently and she had a lonely and bad time, (3) Anne's departure for California because of a Post Commander's threat to extend my tour to a full two years, a threat which followed our somewhat miserable attempt to set up *ad hoc* living arrangements in my room in the Bachelor Officers' Quarters.

"Regular" married life began for us, therefore, about a year and a half after the wedding. And it started then with a cross-country drive to Washington, where I reported for duty and Anne enrolled again in college.

Her resumed schooling put us under fairly severe economic strain (we ate more pea soup for more weeks than is good for any of the bodily functions). But it reflected a feeling we both shared strongly enough to make it a kind of policy: education for either of us came first, and we would pay for it however we had to (and we still have to). Education up to the baccalaureate level was a kind of unquestioned, unevaluated personal necessity for people of our social identification. Beyond that, it was the process required to reach recognized levels of preparation for the head-work, office-type professional occupations we expected to find ful-filling.

And on the subject of occupations and work, Anne and I were indeed well matched. Whereas we tended to carve on each other's egos for sport at home, our approach to the world outside was in tandem. John Calvin's hooks were sunk deep within us both, and we wished to give ourselves to work, to jobs. We both conceived of *employment* as the appropriate condition for adult humans, and that meant employment which satisfied each of us at the same time that it accomplished something we could call productive. From the outset, too, we agreed that both of us would work if we chose, and we left the questions about children and child care to be an-swered at some indefinite future time when we wanted a break from work. (We knew childless couples in my parents' generation, too, both husband and wife employed, whose lives centered on work and seemed happy. We gave serious consideration to emulat-ing their unalloyedly adult lives.)

The agreement that both had the right to occupational satisfac-tion also led, early on, to acceptance of the principle that what we called "system maintenance" functions—shopping, cleaning, etc.—should be equally shared. It took years longer than it should have for me to abandon the final male-claimed prerogatives (for example, not cooking) which prevented full implementation of this principle, but those were years of at least slow progress on the issue, and we had begun at a relatively high level of sharing (I traded other household work for not cooking).

And in terms of occupational focus, we were also in tune. Anne's interests had moved along with mine—often ahead of mine—toward the fields of race and urban problems. She liked the policy and planning aspects more than the human and organizational emphasis which most engaged me, but we were coordinated in our desire to work to make social change—as we were in our intent to find occupations and employing organizations which would enable us to be paid for that work. In fact, before leaving Washington, Anne discovered and did some student work with such an organization, and possibly could have gone on the payroll. But it was agreed that during our next phase together she should support *me* through school (the last year of my Army service was additional to my four obligated years, and I "justified" staying in by the need to pay her tuition—although delaying my departure was actually easier psychologically for me than making the big change).

Thus began an attenuated and seismic process of occupation-educational leapfrogging that carried us almost to our fifteenth wedding anniversary. As we departed for Philadelphia, we were beginning a decade of school ventures, job switches, and diversions into unpaid organizational work that led us all over the income map, but never altered our basic orientation toward employment and productivity. Our lives were organized persistently around our jobs, our studies, our political commitments—our work. First priority for discussion between us: Work. After-hours time needed at the job, or for work at home? Automatic. First Priority. We were joys to our employers. We were high-performance humans, output on demand. And it was largely that fact, along with the concurrence of political belief and a shared sense of humor, which made our relationship cohere.

The transition to the new life was logistically simple—we owned very few things—but emotionally complex, involving a crossover change of roles like a step from some slow minuet.

Anne went from student status to secretarial work, a job—like my Army assignments—not shaped by her influence, and buried in the institutional maze of the university. She did not like it, but she persevered.

I went from orderly institutional employment to the chaos of self-dependent intellectual activity, and almost foundered. I spent extreme amounts of time designing and building (although I didn't know how) pieces of furniture for our apartment.

But the course of study turned out to be quite simple. And even better, by the end of the first year I was hooked up with a budding, large-scale community organization in black North Philadelphia. I combined study with practical work there, always the best way. I began to spend long hours at the organization's offices, getting together leaflets, writing funding proposals. I went to neighborhood protest action meetings about housing problems, lack of income, lack of employment, school inadequacies, police offenses, liquor law abuses, kids on the corner. I became known as a resource connection with the central organization (need a leaflet written and run off? need a bit of research done? a call to some government agency, or supportive on a visit there?). No surprise, when the next grant came through, I was hired—before graduation—as an all-purpose staff member.

Thus I entered the "social change" sector of the job market. It was a growth sector at the time; there was the "war" on poverty beginning, Model Cities programs were in the offing, private foundations were ladling out money, all trying to cool the intense urban ghetto heat created by the interaction of civil rights awakening, the official re-discovery of poverty, and the continuing fact of real impoverishment and worsening living conditions for those who suffered it.

It was an exciting time for young professionals possessed of social consciences—particularly those, like me, whose political understandings had not matured sufficiently to perceive the short circuits hidden in all the new, seemingly progressive energy flow. With so many major and wealthy institutions committed to action, how could there fail to be change? We never really added up the millions proposed for use against the multibillions needed. It took too long for too many of us to understand that even those millions were intended not for poor people themselves, but for people like ourselves who would carry out the grotesque basic policy which held that social services could end economic poverty.

So we went to work with vigor: social workers, planners, lawyers, teachers, and the new species called human relations specialists—my category. For me particularly it was a good time, because I had come back in touch with the proletarian world (subproletarian too, of course, in the big city ghetto), and this time I was bringing something besides my body; I was bringing *help*—information, expertise, organizing guidance, perhaps even, yes, perhaps even the keys to power!!!

So I thought. But gradually, I came to see that the situation was otherwise. While I had arrived most definitely at the social locale of a true mess of problems, the political-economic power and resources to solve those problems were elsewhere. Moreover, I seemed to be doing work which had an underlying effect totally contrary to my intentions. I was (we were) involved in creating the illusions of potential for change while changing nothing. But in the process the programs and activity we generated *diverted* the political attention and energies of people—wage earners and welfare recipients alike—who had to provide the primary impetus for change if it was ever to come. As one of my "nonprofessional" colleagues at the time put it, she and I and all like us were "feeding at the poverty trough."

Sadly, fraudulent dimensions of my work came clearest in the course of my closest reach to direct aid to unemployed wage workers. We were channelling federal on-job training funds into North Philadelphia at a great rate. The program I had designed for the purpose was good, rated high in the region. The staff was aggressive and competent. And the funds were not creating new job opportunities or real skills training at all; they were going as direct subsidies to employers who couldn't get workers otherwise because their working conditions were bad, and to businessmen who *normally* hired in North Philadelphia, off the street, and paid the minimum wage. They treated the regular high turnover rate of disgusted workers as a normal business cost, and were happy to receive the offsetting stipends they got when they committed their marginal jobs to our "training" program. But they were the only employers who would sign on with the program, and the staff had to produce something to justify its paychecks. So we ended up giving aid and comfort to the sleazy but functional part of the economic structure that has always coexisted with urban ghettoes. Its generic name is sweatshop.

It became ever clearer that the power needed to end poverty, remove inequalities, bring justice, all those things, was under control of society's wealth holders—who derived it from ownership of the nation's productive resources and the capital generated by those resources. The power boiled up from the productive core of things where food and fuel and tools and usable things actually appear and begin their circulation, and it was a product of the labor of my life-long protagonists, the wage workers. But as controlled by the owning class, power was being used to sustain the existing social order with all its malformations. The basic prerequisite for true social change more and more defined itself as the acquisition and redistribution of that power. Feeling guilty for my own blindness, I finally became aware of the enormity of the contradiction involved in a putative democratic system which exempts from democratic control the largest single influence in the life of the nation and its citizens—the economy.

So, by halts and jerks, and at first sorrowfully, I crossed the line into racial territory. I could no longer deny that the needed process of social change had to begin (or at least join early on) with the substitution of socialism for capitalism. And if my intent in employment was to work for such change, I obviously belonged in some politically functional connection with the productive core rather than my current Patagonian position, chasing and raging at the thin fallout of power and benefits on this furthest periphery away. But at that point I knew too little to understand that I might be employable (professionally speaking, that is) by, for instance, a labor union. And I had avoided the hard transaction professions—law, for example, or medicine, education, communications, science—that might have enabled me to move closer in.

Moreover, the political and occupational distance from my point of desired involvement was only accentuated by the social distance that had opened as Anne and I succeeded in advancing our careers. As soon as I had steady salary coming in, she had begun graduate studies in urban planning. And when the economic balance allowed, she had quit her unwanted job (where, of course, she was earning plaudits). She had been hired by a prestigious private housing advocacy organization, an energetic and evolving holdover from the settlement house era. She was rising with it toward administrative rank, as was I in my increasingly institutionalized, program-operating community organization. I was still an all-purpose staff worker (although the skin-color factor increasingly negated my potential for neighborhood contact work), but my adeptness at writing funding proposals had brought in many more staff people who were mostly paid less and ranked lower than me.

Combined, Anne's income and mine gave us more money than we had (or have) ever had at one time. We were working hard, validating each other's work (although my uptown, black-controlled organization gave me the edge on her in liberal chic, and I used it when we discussed local politics and program strategies). We lived well, in expensive downtown apartments. We acquired furniture, a car. I had suits to wear and so did she. We consorted with other young professionals. And reveling in our output of energy and devotion to duty, we continued to postpone the decision about whether to have children.

Anne was also going through political changes, and they were similar to mine. (We shared the process, of course, but eventually took different directions from it). And gradually it became impossible to manage the contradictions in which we found ourselves. The contrasts between the locations and lives we sought to aid through our work, and the location and style of our own life, became too great. The logic of our political beliefs finally asserted full claim on our self-respect, and demanded that we find other ways to work, and to try to exemplify the patterns of social and economic sharing we wished for the world at large.

By the time of our eighth wedding anniversary, we had left our jobs, moved into a commune, and were engaged heavily in an organization called People for Human Rights (PHR, a chapter of the national People Against Racism), which espoused and took direct action on the racial and economic fronts.

Changes in our income and life style were severe. And they were accompanied by a considerable amount of occupational rethinking and fresh starting.

But unlike several younger friends who were going through the same sort of transitional experience, trying to make political sense of their lives and work, our changes all took place within the context of our established social status and identity. Those others, with whom we shared political convictions and organizational affiliations, opted for immersion in the working-class world through jobs in factories and service work. They are still there.

I was not quite able to countenance such a step, and the idea was essentially inconceivable to Anne. Nor were we able to accept the idea, as some others did, of long-term voluntary impoverishment while lending our so-called professional skills—writing, budgeting, research, etc.—to the support efforts which would make the organizing work of these class-line crossers more effective.

We had some ideological support for our reluctance; it was a time when "New Working Class" theories, now somewhat faded, were in vogue. It seemed as though all the young professionals—at least those institutionally employed—were going to be able to claim equivalent status of exploitation with the industrial and service work force. It seemed as though political organizing among these higher-paid, nonproletarian workers was going to be a *right way* to proceed.

Some of this theoretical conception was quite accurate: note, for instance, that the fastest increase in unionization over the last ten years has been among teachers and other professional-level government and private-sector white-collar workers formerly viewed (and self-described) as beyond the pale of organized labor. But in the rush to form new world views incorporating this anticipated spread of "proletarianization" of professional occupations and their practitioners (which, of course, ain't exactly what happened), it was all too convenient to forget that the central and largest part of the working class remained in the wage-grade service and industrial production sectors which would necessarily be the prime element of any significant movement to make over the political-economic system. A teachers' strike can have strong effects—children losing education, family life disrupted—but it has no significant impact on the economy outside the educational institution involved. When workers in steel, coal, oil, or communications strike, however, other basic parts of the national mechanism begin to shut down.

Of course, "New Working Class" or not, it was and is not necessary to be a wage worker in order to push for socialism, or even to advocate the spread of progressive organization among wage workers. But what would Anne and I do? We had no special gifts to offer, no recondite skills. Our professional capacities had no match with pre-established occupational categories of need outside the limited field of social change organizations and related institutions. Even if we were to do political work among white-collar types, we would be better off taking routinized jobs in the lower-paid sectors of the bureaucracy.

But we valued the mental independence and the range of creativity and initiative afforded by our jobs thus far. We did not want jobs that we did not like. We wanted *satisfying* work. Moreover, we were too thoroughly formed in habit to seriously contemplate a complete revision of life style; we were, and are, wards of the social conventions and tastes and bodily comforts of our upbringings and recent years of marriage.

So it was that an even more significant cushion for our reorientation process, stronger than any political theories, was the fact that in our commune, those conventions and tastes and comforts were normal. It was ironic: the commune was radically different from our past living situation and experiences, and so (truly) showed our wish and willingness to be involved in collective endeavor and reshaped social arrangements. But it was also so bourgeois and so affluent that it obviated the need to question the validity of our essentially horizontal social transition.

At most times the communal house (a huge derelict edifice in a low-income brown/black/white neighborhood, which we collectively rehabilitated) held six or seven people, and operated with three above-median incomes. There was another couple besides us, both employed as social workers; their son, age five; and a fifth adult who sometimes shared company with a sixth. Costs of operation were apportioned by ability to pay, except in the case of the fifth adult—that "slot" in the house was reserved for someone doing political work for low or no pay, and the house sustained that person's room and board as a political commitment. (Other aspects of life there were fairly standard for a commune: cleaning, cooking, and child care were shared equally on rotation. Dinner was the communal meal. House meetings were held to set budgets, decide points of policy, and deal with problems.)

Anne was the one adult of the basic four who brought in no wages. She was in an uncharacteristically directionless lull. She had begun to feel uncomfortable dissonance in her effort to integrate her employment and her political sentiments, so while she continued with political activity in PHR and a women's group, she experimented with personal expression as a means of occupational fulfillment: writing, photography, gardening. (Notably, occupational fulfillment was a goal sufficiently valued by our social-peer communards that they willingly subsidized her experiments.) But she found these removed and introspective activities unsatisfying. Her search for an employment which would satisfy her work and skill capacities without necessarily demanding an overlap with her political life led her eventually to library administration. But in the meantime, she went with the Venceremos Brigade to socialist Cuba, where for six weeks she planted and harvested citrus.

Occupationally, I moved in the other direction. (The expanded social-emotional involvements of the commune reduced the intense interdependencies and dominations of our marital relationship, allowing this basic divergence to take place while we remained together, adjusting.) I had become imbued with the luxurious notion that my work should engage and employ all my primary interests and my political convictions as well as my training and capabilities.

This is a notion that operates on the universe of job possibilities as tides treat your sand castle. It is the main reason that I am now a freelance writer. But at the time, I managed to find a job— a ridiculous job in terms of scope, but engrossing. And true to form and past binding, it was in the field of social change. It was a program funded by a church organization that set me and a women's movement organizer shuttling (usually separately) around the nine-county Philadelphia metropolitan. We were to get white suburbanites ("New Working Class" at home?) organized and involved in trying to change their own and others' attitudes on race and sex and authority. I managed to get a couple of local bail funds under way, but otherwise the rubber and oil I left on the roads were the only evidence of my passage.

Among other things, however, this job used my work time differently than ever before—I had spurts of intense activity, then spaces of relaxation. I put many of the resulting spare hours into PHR work, but Anne and I still often found ourselves in an unusual position; home together in the daytime on weekdays, with no demands from work to occupy us. This sort of break from all the recent years of striving and exhaustion invited back The Big Question: whether or not to have children.

In previous discussions, Anne typically had proposed having children—even though she was willing to postpone the deed itself—and I opposed (no time! curtailed flexibility! emotional drain!). But with her own occupational situation now so open, she was no longer willing to postpone. Even with my own more flexible work life, I found I was unwilling to commit myself to the future kid prospect. My interests and involvements and desires were so outward oriented, and there had been so many years in which that pattern was the mutual first value of our relationship, that the idea of expanding my homebound responsibilities and familial emotional connections was painful.

But Anne's pressure for agreement was strong and growing. And at the same time, another source of positive pressure was developing from a completely different direction. Men's consciousness groups had formed in PHR in its latter days, and I was in one. Raising the issue there, I got back the strong suggestion that I might absorb a considerable amount of information about humanity and love by involving myself in the nurture of children. I could not accept that as a bald surety, particularly as it was urged most strongly by some of the childless men in the group. But I was also trying to persuade myself by then—it was apparent that continued marriage with Anne depended on agreement, and neither of us wanted the relationship to end (even though we sometimes wished it would disappear). So, I found a sticking point for myself on the fact that while childlessness might not deny a good life, it did prevent access to a large and important sector of human experience—some of which quite probably would be valuable as described by the men's group.

So I bottled my resistance, but did not extinguish it. Nor have I ever completely done so. Thinking about our son Nick, now seven, I am glad that I made the positive decision. It was right, Anne was right. But it was also helplessly wrong; no amount of added human experience can remove the fact that the desire for employment, for adult occupation, and the wish to use strength and energy in work (other than daycare, of course) do not mix well with the raising of children.

At any rate, we then came up against the anticlimactic fact that biologically we could not conceive a child. So we began proceedings to adopt, a drawn-out proposition. And by the time Nick arrived, three years later, much in the evolving equation of life and work was changed for us. We lived in Boston by then, and we were back in an apartment by ourselves. And our involvements and investments in our occupations were both different and divergent.

The move to Boston—which dealt the commune a serious but temporary injury—came because of the best job I expect ever to have. Friends had invited me to apply for (and I got) the position of head administrator of a thirty-person organization offering technical assistance, organizing support, and research backup to community and workplace groups in industrial communities in Eastern Massachusetts. (It specialized in issues such as housing, transportation, occupational health and safety, and access to media.)

Of all the politically intended professional organizations I have encountered, this one made the greatest effort, and had the greatest success, in functionally involving its services in the growth of working class political strength. In fact, it was that effort which gave the organization its primary conceptual coherence.

But the organization also had a social coherence which was warm and rewarding. The operating structure there was based on collective responsibility; there was no hierarchy of power, no clerical-professional status divisions (everyone did their own secretarial work, and organizational output was amazingly high). While I was there we finally got the salary system rationalized into an equal base pay all around with additions for dependents and other preset categories of need. This meant that the highest paid staff member was not me, the putative Executive Director, but a divorced female tenant organizer with three children. Moreover, organizational policy decisions and work plans were collectively made and collectively evaluated.

I basked, we all basked as we worked. Most people in the organization were so excited and engrossed by what we had that talk amongst one another was of little else than the organization and its affairs. (Spouses—including Anne—complained about this and resented it.) We were all fairly young, mostly college- or university-trained, competent, and politically Leftist—although there were many varieties of left-wing attachment. And we were sharing a high-energy work experience that seemed to be putting us all to best purpose as individuals and as a collective group. Marvelous.

Also exhausting. There was the predictable, continuing load of personnel tensions (no organizational structure avoids them), and they were my responsibility—at one level or another—to adjust.

Baby Nicholas had arrived, and Anne cared for him alone during the daytime hours of his first months with us. But she had already been accepted by the graduate school she had chosen for her work toward a library science degree, and her classes soon began. My efforts to secure a rationalized pay system at my organization at that time were bringing about a reduction in my salary, which she resented. And for my part I resented the claims on my time imposed by the need to share child care with her during my prized working hours after her schoolwork started.

I was accustomed, for instance, to wind up my work day in relaxed, supportive discussions with others in the organization who lingered for the same purpose, or by clearing up detail work as the offices emptied out and became silent. It was usually a half-hour to an hour after official closing time before I went home, and I liked and valued that extension of my time at the desk, in the chair. I liked my work so much, in fact, that it was of happy significance just to be where it took place—to sit and look around at the furnishings, as familiar as those at home, redolent of the experiences of the day and of the continuing emotional satisfactions of the job. I soaked it in. And I closed the door each evening, even after days of tension and frustration, with a small feeling of regret.

But now Anne's class schedule required that I leave promptly at ten minutes before five to pick up Nick at the day-care center. Ant that was not all: the center was an infant-care operation that we and other parents had had to organize. It had one paid teacher (all we could support), and otherwise depended on parent work participation. Anne and I each spent one-half day a week there as teacher's assistants. More time gone. And try as I might, I could not develop an enthusiasm for the child care work to make up for my sense of loss at being away from my beloved organization.

Subliminally, however, pressure was also building in my own psyche to move away from that organization, any organization, for a while. I had worked ten years in various group endeavors, pursuing goals which realistically were beyond the competence of anything but a mass movement. There was a growing insistence within me that I should spend some time isolating and asserting myself as a self.

Among other things, it was clear that I had come about as close as I ever could to the ideal of productive, outsider-professional involvement with the politically progressive salients of the working class. But the ideal, when reached, was less satisfying in some respects than it should have been. It was not good enough to remain an outsider; providing technical assistance, regardless how valuable, did not create continuing social relationships with the people and organizations I wanted to join in movement. And how *productive* was this sort of work anyway? How could I hope to know its real productivity if I was so distant from the social locale of its effects?

Mainly, however, I lacked the mental and emotional energy to go on trying to figure such things out. The idea of writing as an occupation had reasserted itself—in college days I had dreamed of it (that is, I had dreamed of being a famous and respected writer). Removal—removal to write—seemed likely to free me for a new period of reconsideration about work, and about family. I needed to find better ways to adapt myself, emotionally as well as in scheduling, to my son's growth and care.

And lo and behold, there was a magic suddenly in the idea that for some undefined period I might not work directly with other people—that I might escape the daily puzzles of human relationships at work, and the head-against-wall effort of trying to apply my work repetitively, organizationally, and still creatively to the process of social transformation.

It is, after all, a taxing sort of situation, helplessly to experience daily life's inexorable immersion in routines, traditions, and institutions of the culture and society you are working to change; like trying to change clothes and stay dressed at the same time. (With the home pressures wrapped in to boot, I had developed a pre-ulcerous stomach, and was on medication.) Radical critics who are outside the central core of commerce and production circle that center like hungry ghosts. They long for the time when they will be able—morally, politically, emotionally—to enjoy and participate in the everyday processes of society without constant questions and criticisms. But the prerequisite for such immersion (short of simple loss of energy) is that society alter itself so as to be clearly progressing, equalizing itself, improving the lot of its least-favored members.

At least that is how I felt and feel. I wish to be able to produce for the collective good, and take pride in the effort, and feel with my fellow citizens an equality of responsibility and benefit. I envy but cannot join those who find such satisfactions in present political-economic arrangements, or who presume them to be there (whether experienced or not), and never seek anything different.

It seemed, however, that I might take the luxury of joining—however temporarily—those who communicate such thoughts in the removed form of print rather than in direct interchange with allies and opponents.

So we agreed to shift again, and this time to shift not only from my earnings to Anne's, but from the urban places where we had spent so much time and effort to a country setting of some sort. We had foolish images of how calming that might be. I would write (smoke a pipe? wear a cardigan?); Anne would experience the satisfactions of entering her salaried working life in her new job field in some friendly, manageably-sized library; our son would gambol in daisy fields.

She got the requisite job, and we moved to the requisite place, and there were fields of hawkweed if not daisies. It was esthetically pleasant. But inside, the emotions churned on. Writing turned out to be *hard* work, with few gratifications for the learner (I had not expected to be a learner). And the daily encounter with the sense of responsibility to act politically never abated. How could it? I tried to find ways to write politically, and to use my writing for political purposes, but the results were clumsy at first and did not sell.

I was doing even more child care, of course—one or two mornings a week in the parent-run playgroup (again, we had to organize it), and afternoons between the end of Nick's nap and Anne's return. Despite my best intentions, that palled. I longed for clear work time, even though I was not sure what I could do with it. The pre-ulcerous stomach condition cropped up again.

With it came the panic: what hideous mistake had I made? Abandoning my "career line," trotting off to this cow town, pushing thirty-seven years old by then with no viable occupation. Alumni magazines came, revealing that all college classmates had become corporate vice-presidents, military colonels, or esteemed professors.

It was eighteen months before the first sale of any of my work, and another six months before the next. Confidence stretched mighty thin. Then we moved, three years ago, Anne going on up her career ladder. We live in a larger town, closer to Boston, but still far from it. But it is near to some smaller urban centers, which made me start thinking about reversing my course. But the results were a disaster. After settling in, I went after an executive-level job being advertised in a social-change agency. I didn't even make the interview list. A year later, I made the same attempt again, even though my writing had begun selling consistently: the lack of a steady-earning, steady-producing job, daily out of the house, paycheck every week, fellow workers to talk to, all of that, still generated an unshakable background anxiety. But the second attempt also failed: among the finalists, I was not the final choice for hire. Double rejection! No exits left.

So I continued—and continue—working with words. Sometimes it seems fruitful to do so. Sometimes it seems so abstract that I quit for a stint at some wage-grade job (a pickle factory last time), which of course also becomes "material" for writing. I have new knowledge, I learn many things as I research the variety of topics and issues I have to turn into articles. I interview other people about their work and I find examples, sometimes, that make me think "would this have been better?" (The maintenance worker in a local foundry, for instance, who explained to me in detail during one conversation that the difference between his work and mine was not as between head and hand; that he planned, improvised, imagined, invented, as well as using his tools—all in the process of ensuring production of basic, indispensable metal.)

I know that words are indispensable too, but whether or not mine are indispensable remains a question more open than I would like to have it. As my own production has increased, the quality improving, my discontent has eased out of the true cellars of worry. My writing is politically satisfactory much of the time, and has in fact done more than any other work in my life to close the gap my girlfriend's mother spotted so long ago. Responses to newspaper features I have written on workplace issues and workers' history give me now a greater sense than ever before that my professional occupation is communicating my political perspective to the working-class people I wish to address, with whom I wish to associate and move for change. I also have organizational involvements which employ my political energies.

But it is a manic-depressive life. Each piece of work sold is a lift (although, like dope, it increasingly takes either more or bigger sales to attain a repeat of the same elevation). And each rejection, or inability to think for a day, or ridiculous draft that looked okay the night before, opens up some part of those large-scale questions: have I failed, or does it just feel that way? Why have I not risen like my classmates to become a man of mark—a radical man of mark? How come my wife managed to find her way to a career which satisfies her, which pays her tolerable money for regular work, and in which she gets to advance and be respected, while I take deliveries of manure from editors and potter about with where to put words in a sentence?

And will this work be acceptable and satisfying when—and until—I am sixty-five?

Why in God's name don't I have a job? I think I will leave this here and go and have a drink.

Afterwords:
An Eight-way
Conversation

collated by Peter Filene

We wrote our essays without knowing whether they would ever be published. Each of us contributed a piece to what became, piece by piece, a whole manuscript, but not until we had finished did we know for sure that the manuscript would become a book. Most of us, I suspect, wrote for ourselves and our friends—statements more private than public. But now a publisher has said "Yes," and our private lives will be put into the hands of strangers. Suddenly we look upon these pages in a new light. As Steve Turner confessed in a recent letter: "I freeze up a little at the thought that the personal story I've written is about to become public. Will people think me ridiculous? Self-important? Why am I in this book?"

On the eve of opening night, as second thoughts come like fever chills, the eight of us decided to take a last look at ourselves, or really two last looks. First, each of us reread his own essay, looking over the shoulder of one or two years' hindsight in order to ask: How much do I still agree with the perspectives I had then? What do I see now that I overlooked then? And how do I bring my story up to date? Second, we read the other seven essays, in effect introducing ourselves to one another. I have known all the contributors personally, but most of them know each other only through these pages. By responding to the neighboring essays, they truly shape the pieces into a collective product. I have collated their written reactions into a kind of conversation, chiming in occasionally with my own remarks, but otherwise serving as the host of a seven-man talk show.

Reviewing One's Self-Portrait

"Writing such a thing is hard enough," says Tom Kreilkamp, "but rereading it after time has passed . . . now, that's truly difficult." Despite embarrassment, shocks of recognition, and a myriad of other feelings and excuses, however, we managed to look back at the "thing" we had rendered of our experiences with work and family.

ARN STRASSER: In these two years I feel I have walked too often on the edge of the pit marked "DANGER: Obsession with Work." The challenge of keeping my life in balance is a constant one. "It's a shame," said William Faulkner, "that there is so much work in the world. One of the saddest things is that the only thing a man can do for eight hours a day, day after day, is work." So I fight the urge to take work home, and try to head for my drawing board instead. What I have been able to do is to set aside a certain time each week to draw. This schedule has produced, I am pleased to say, my first set of coherent drawings.

What I am also pleased with is how much I enjoy my work, even if it does seem very threatening sometimes. A doctor's work is a privileged work, allowing a special relationship with many different kinds of people of all ages. It is never tedious and always challenging. The frustration comes for me primarily in demons called accounts receivable and bills and petty vandalism. I have wanted so badly to succeed in the past two years and as a result have had to face a theme of these essays: just what is success and why do we middle-class white men want it with such an especially burning ferocity? The matter came to a focus for me this winter when I was sick with the flu and each time I came out of the fever I was thinking of the clinic. I ended up at a doctor friend of mine, my chiropractor, and I sat in the room and cried and cried—the tension of the sickness and the frustrations of the clinic coming out. He told me it was Pride (pride of the doctor getting sick) that I had to let go of and that I had to stop trying to be something I wasn't. "Find out who you are and practice that way. You can't 'please' people. And what would you do with success anyway?"

My marriage has ended. I feel it was a painful victory, but a victory nevertheless. After four years of school (my tenth year of college!) and then a year struggling to open the clinic came the intense experience of child and marriage. We had our birth at home, with Blair arriving to a circle of friends, my tears of joy and so close to Diane, seeing deep into her eyes. But the closeness never could hide our differences and the many ways which, despite love and intimacy, our marriage wasn't working. The victory came in that breaking away, against considerable resistance. And that is a kind of liberation to say "I don't have to sacrifice myself. If it isn't working, really isn't, then I am not obligated, whether to marriage or to work."

The marriage has ended, but family continues. For me it's the life of the single parent. Packing lunches, "Dharma *please* clean this room," and "god, what about my own room, laundry again," "good meal, huh?" oh shit, how can this place be in such chaos again, laughter, music, school report on aphids. . . . Diane and I continue trying to fashion a relationship that works. I see Blair a few times a month. Marian and I are by now old hands at shared child care and are good, if vulnerable, friends.

I don't feel that the changes in my life have been "random." Many have been quite deliberate, though they may come from voices deep inside me which I try to coax to the surface. I am questioning what I am doing, and why I am doing it. The process is not smooth or coldly logical. Nothing of the kind. It's fraught with delusion, of course. But I feel as if I relate decisions to a developing personal philosophy grounded in the seminal period of my life, the "sixties," and guided by a jarring series of mistakes. It is interesting to me now, with that period even further from today's reality, that I turned so easily to the autobiographical title "child of the sixties." Sometimes this puts me out of step with the other essayists. I feel more romantic or idealistic.

From Michael and Marian, I learn about jealousy. From broken marriage, I discover myself again. From "why can't I have more patients," I learn about pride. All this is embarrassingly personal, and middle class, compared to being laid off a job or being hungry. Yet I feel that men who have questioned the past male prerogatives should feel pride. I feel this pride and I look forward to more changes and I simply refuse to be downbeat about it.

LAWRENCE RUBIN: The climax of my essay focused on the leisurely rhythm that I had found at last for my life. Since then, our son Noah was born and he has shot the rhythm all to hell. Time has been completely transformed around his needs, day and night. Once I could play golf a few times a week, do a little fishing. But no more.

The most significant consequence has been the partial redefinition of the relationship with my wife. We are constantly asking ourselves, "who's responsible for what?" Our answer is to share responsibilities, but in no rigidly spelled-out formula. So we go through an intense daily process of spelling out what each of us is responsible for. The process is particularly necessary and intense because Elizabeth is an artist and needs privacy; she needs time in her own right. In my essay I talked about conflict and compromise in what I thought were strong terms. But believe me, the original essay is just chicken feed compared to what we are going through now.

Business, I'm happy to report, has been good the last couple of years. The connection with Brazil is still tenuous and exasperating at times. But by constant effort and some good breaks I've managed to establish a fairly profitable (though of course never dependable) volume of sales.

ROBERT HAHN: I was thirty-nine when I wrote my piece, and I have now crossed the divide of forty. Last Christmas my wife and I separated. For half a year I have lived (along with my thirteen-year-old son) the life of a single parent, a single man. Meanwhile, I am completing a master's program in educational administration, and also working as director of a continuing education program, a pair of responsibilities which create a work week of fifty hours or more.

Paul Fiddleman's remark on "the randomness of so much that happens to us" joins Kreilkamp's *only connect* to suggest a central theme in our essays: the attempt to connect—not only the poetry and the prose, the present and the past—to connect the decision points in our lives into a coherent pattern. But they don't connect because the decisions are less rational and reasoned than we think. Often they are driven by forces we don't comprehend; often they are more impulsive, simplistic, or starkly expedient than we can acknowledge.

There is a truth here I find more powerful than any number of testimonials to mature, cooperative homemaking. I am moved by the violent eruptions of that truth in the unhappy saga of Michael and Marian in Strasser's essay and in the unforeseen end of Filene's second marriage. The heavens are blank, and the world bristles with comic demons. Part of the meaning of the late 60s is that the times gave an external shape to our devils. Now we are back in the soup again, tailing out of the Me Generation, obsessed with money and housing, still thinking (for some reason) it is important to confront our feelings, but often unsure what lies beyond.

HARRY BOYTE: Reading my essay, I find it terribly deficient in dealing with "normal" anxieties, fears, insecurities about career, and the judgment of others, etc. I recognize this deficiency only now, after struggling to come to terms with my history, fantasies, and reality during the last year and a half. One would certainly not get from my essay the message that I was about to have a very serious drinking problem, or that I was to go through two years of torment about the book I was writing, or that I would try to rework the intellectual edifice of the left-wing tradition. None of this comes through.

The fact is that I was left with unbelievable, ridiculous expectations from my father and mother, and myself. My father didn't only make up songs about my future; he thought I would be president (senator would be only halfway making it); my mother thought I would be another Laski or Malinowski. And some of my teachers fed these kinds of fantasies, often considering me not only bright, but a genius. In college I rebelled with ferocity . . . but also accepted the expectations. I was a rebel from normal career patterns (following and deviating from my father's dreams, but functioning in a similarly grandiose way). I couldn't *allow* myself normal career patterns; that would have felt like selling out for the sake of approval. But I felt that survival itself depended on incredible success. So in form and content I saw myself as some kind of Lenin/Marx . . . in a country where the Left was marginal, and largely illusion. And all the while I was terrified that, through some quirk, my grandiose fantasies might come "true." I might become famous, and believe in myself as seen through the image of my fame.

It all led to a terrible, ridiculous, and tortured decade for me, to a great deal of trouble in my relationship with Sara, and ultimately to a kind of breaking free, a change in my values, an intense search for "real" roots in my life. Specifically: rebuilding relations with Sara and Craig; Al Anon; counseling; flickerings of religious faith, after more than a decade of firm agnosticism. With all of this has also come more acceptance of my needs for success as well as for making a contribution with integrity and self-respect. I also recognize, finally, that my grandiosity will never really "go away." It is a driving force that scares me deeply, but that I can control (when I let myself understand).

PETER FILENE: I have mixed feelings after reading my essay and emerging on those last pages, which were written in the wake of my father's death and my wife's departure. I feel glad to have grown past that long winter filled with so much anguish and anger and uncertainty. Yet I know that I am far from fully understanding what happened either in my second marriage or in my work. I have spent the last year trying to make sense of the past while also making a more gratifying present.

Despite impulses to flee to a new job, a new city, a new life, I stayed where I was. And in the all-too-familiar locale of Chapel Hill I discovered new ways of enjoying myself. Most important, I began telling people "I'm a photographer as well as a teacher." The paralyzing bind of "either/or" in career suddenly dissolved.

While taking a summerschool course in advanced photography, I spent the early afternoon in class, the late afternoon shooting at least two rolls, the evening in the darkroom developing and printing until midnight or later, the night (literally) dreaming of black and white images coming up in trays of Dektol, and the morning contemplating my contact sheets. Coaxed by the gentle and shrewd appreciations of my teacher, John Menapace, I came out of the course with a sense of a possibility of a visual style. And ever since I've been nurturing that sense, like a hard candy tucked in my cheek. Writing poems brought heroic pain; making photographs brings pleasure without any impulse to "prove" something or "succeed." That much I know for sure. I'm not at all sure why most of my pictures have been of small children, large shadows, and deep spaces. But I don't want to analyze; I trust intuition now.

My teaching schedule provides a luxurious amount of free time, which I have used in happy ways. Roller skating across campus. Jogging. Motorcycling. Dancing, a lot of dancing. Quiet times for musing, free associating. Flute lessons. Two or three evenings a week with Benjamin and Becky, sometimes more and sometimes less, but always precious. Innumerable letters, phone calls, and casual meals with friends. And also "dating," so ludicrously young a word for a not-so-young man, but that's what I've done, including a number of blind dates that turned out less disastrously than one would have expected and that in any case honed my wry humor about midlife madness. A lot of dates, some romantic flurries, one relationship of several serious months, and more false hopes than I like to remember.

During this year, I've begun to trust my inner resources. I can depend upon myself to travel through open space and find lively surprises. But I also veer into old cul-de-sacs. Sometimes I hear the siren call of "hurry up and succeed," and I feel as if my activities are "pointless." Sometimes I am enchanted by the aura of some beautiful, intelligent woman and I believe for a week, "you will make me safe and happy." Fortunately at the beginning of each new week my therapy group helps me clarify what is out there and what is in me, and then what in me is truly what I want rather than what I delude myself into believing.

STEVE TURNER: I'm moving to Lowell, Massachusetts, where Anne is the new City Library Director. She is already working there, coming home on weekends, and Nick and I will join her when his school is done. I'm not sure what will happen to me then—maybe I actually *will* get a job. On the other hand, I'm fishing with a friend for a grant to do a labor history film, which would be a nice change. In any case, I expect I'll keep writing for a while.

PAUL FIDDLEMAN: In looking over the essay after a two-year period, I can honestly say that very little has changed during that period of time, at least in terms of objective characteristics. I am still comfortably married, my children are growing older, my job remains the same except for some additional areas of consultation, I am a bit grayer of head and a bit heavier. In fact, the changes that have impacted are the ones that have occurred to important others in my life.

The major change is that my children, particularly the oldest, are growing up and in many ways I am saddened by it. They have moved more and more into contact with others, and while we are still important to them, our importance has diminished as their investments have increased in others. Perhaps the most sobering thought is that in two years my "baby girl" will be gone from the house. She will have graduated from high school and gone on, either to college or to something or someone else. I feel a sense of urgency; there is so much that we haven't told her or prepared her for, and there is so very little time. I can tell parents of patients that they have done all they can in terms of building character, values, beliefs, and options; the best they can now do is break the bottle of champagne over their children's bow and turn them loose. Easy for me to say about someone else, much harder for me to feel good about.

Unlike me, who has comfortably fit into my job and realize that any real advancement will be an internal one, my wife's situation is different. She has grown into an effective clinician, working in the demanding intensive care program and, in the past three years, become the second highest person on the staff. This summer she has taken a three-month leave of absence in order to check out what values the housewife role holds for her, and also to spend time with our daughter. I am impressed with that decision, and even more with her decision to become more involved with her weaving. She is a weaver, has begun to show some work, and will attend a two-week advanced-weaving course at the Penland School of Crafts. This gives her something that I wish I had developed: a hobby. I have no hobby and would like to develop one. In looking at the essay I noted the lack of real leisure-time activities that were mine rather than oriented around my family. In a few years I will have to perform my leisure on my own.

The other issue which arises in looking over the essay is power. I have always been somewhat uncomfortable with the use of power. Although I can enjoy reducing a hostile, authoritarian, s.o.b. to rubble, particularly in the name of a worthy cause, I recognize the enjoyment and am wary of it. Far more dangerous, I think, is the fact that I can so easily become the provider of profound truths in my consulting activities. I have not enjoyed seeing other professional consultants display their power needs, and I hope I remain sensitive to this somewhat dark side of myself.

The other side of power is vulnerability. I feel this other side intrusively at the moment as I sit here after pulling large muscles in both calves during a father-son baseball game. They always say your legs go first, but having had to limp off first base for a pinch runner because I couldn't run on my own is a bit ego-deflating. I have also become aware that, in writing the essay, I totally ignored (repressed, denied, suppressed) a bout with illness when I was forty. It was later diagnosed as ulcerative colitis, it lasted about two months, and it managed to scare the living shit out of me. I had never been sick before, and it was a terrifying experience.

I don't like to be vulnerable. I have learned to be adept enough to avoid getting into vulnerable situations in my work. But I am consistently bothered by my vulnerability about the kids, and by the fact that their hurts hurt me. They handle the day-to-day difficulties that most youngsters encounter, and they handle them well. Yet I still suffer, more than I want to, when they encounter pain. They are my only Achilles heel at this time.

TOM KREILKAMP: I do not find new meanings in my own essay a year or two later. My life has changed, but not in ways that would lead me to significantly alter what I wrote. For example, when I finished the essay I was still engaged in training for a new career. Now I have entered that career and it is clearly a good one for me. I have changed from full-time teaching to virtually full-time therapy. Because I miss teaching, however, I have chosen to do one course a year at Harvard. This teaching is unpaid, by the way, but it is still part of my "career" in some sense or another. Thus, all my worst fears about not being able to get jobs, or about having to move in order to find them, turn out to be groundless. Moreover, throughout this change from teaching to therapy, I have retained a sense of myself supporting my family and me in ways that involve some pleasure, some sense of doing good (or at least avoiding harm), some stimulation, even some joy. There has been no sense of a break with my past.

Vera and I have adjusted to my new work life. This is the fourth year in a row that I have been out of the house forty hours or more each week, a schedule which has put more pressure on Vera at home and more reliance on child care help. Thus far, however, things have been going smoothly—so smoothly, in fact, that Vera is thinking of working full time next year in her teaching job.

Looking at Ourselves
Collectively

RECOGNITIONS   As the contributors read one another's essays, they expressed diverse responses. "I recognize some of these men very well," Paul Fiddleman reports. "In fact, some of them at times actually, physically existed in my space, although often on opposite sides of the barricades." He and I both grew up in New York City during the 1940s, Fiddleman notes, but he was on the Brooklyn street-smart, ethnic, fight-to-save-your-ass side, while I was on the Manhattan bourgeois, intellectual side "skating around the traffic." Likewise, he and Harry Boyte both worked with ACT, the Durham community-organizing agency, but Fiddleman stayed on the periphery as a skeptical adviser while Boyte worked wholeheartedly in the center. "I am struck," Fiddleman says, "with how all the essayists shared the same conflicts and crises, but how markedly we all differed in our personal commitment to these issues and in our resolution of them."

For the most part, then, he recognizes differences. But while reading Tom Kreilkamp's essay "I found myself nodding: yeah, yeah, that's the way it is. He and I share the same profession, maintain long-term marriages with people who are very different from each of us, and have little heavy investment in success as it is defined by our peers." Kreilkamp, in turn, writes: "I found myself identifying most of all with Fiddleman's essay. I think the reason is less the coincidence that we are both clinical psychologists, and more a matter of tone. His pages have less of a sense of groping for some unreachable goals. Instead, I detect a sense of settledness which is not dull rigidity but rather a kind of acceptance of certain of life's limitations. I don't think it is the outcome of his essay with which I identify; again, it's more the tone. Perhaps it's a 'taking' of a career and a life and a family without being totally absorbed by them."

For Steve Turner, "the most succinct, evocative presentation of basic shared content came in Robert Hahn's wry but lovely image of men working in trees. Which branch to choose? How high to climb? Does it matter if there's only empty air underneath? In the same vein, one might talk about spousal relationships working in trees."

And Hahn moves his metaphor down to ground level: "Hearing my cohorts talk about themselves is like a walk through a house of mirrors where the distortions are more or less recognizable images of oneself. When Boyte talks of his father, I realize I didn't deal with mine at all, perhaps because he was a powerful god in the process of being appeased by my quest for a more respectable line of work. Fiddleman's insights about the 50s illuminate my own experience, and his focus on the blind quality of early decisions is apt."

So we have found that coincidence, or tone, or philosophy makes alliances among us. And sometimes coincidence allies us without our knowing. Neither Hahn nor Strasser was aware that, since completing their essays, both of them had undergone a sudden and painful dissolution of their marriages. All the more poignantly ironic, then, to hear Strasser say, "I feel an unusual closeness to these men. As a man I usually feel isolated from other men. The true-to-the-heart friend, defenses down, vulnerability and triumph revealed, is the exception. Mostly I hide, we hide, behind our man-talk. It is so refreshing, then, to read what the eight of us have attempted. Eight voices trying to break out of the mantalk, trying to break out of the manshell. I feel comfortable in this circle of voices."

Well, nothing so neat as a circle unites the eight of us. A ragged circle perhaps. Or several irregular loops. Or should we picture ourselves on eight separate branches of a tree? In any case, one fact is clear: we feel that we belong together in one book, because we recognize so much of what has happened in one another's work and family.

MISSING BODIES   If we make recognitions, we also see disguises. "What's missing?" Strasser asks. "Our physical bodies: how do we look and how do we move? And our sexuality: when did we first masturbate and what are, or have been, our sexual fears and fantasies?"

We are indeed very silent about sexuality. Except for an occasional terse reference to going to bed with a woman, usually his wife, none of the essayists undresses himself on these pages. Masturbation, homosexuality, impotence, and other sexual topics go unmentioned. When I asked my fellow contributors about their silence, they had ready explanations. "Although the essayists do not talk about their sex lives," Hahn replied, "they talk, indeed talk quite obsessively, about their loves and their affairs. This emphasis is related to their middle-class natures. After all, when was the last time you and I sat down and had an intimate talk about experiences in bed with our women?"

As for impotence, none of us voiced concern with this topic. Either we have never experienced it or we consider it symptomatic of the much larger version of the potency question: namely, how well do we cope with our status, power, or efficacy beyond the bedroom? And specifically on the matter of bisexuality, Fiddleman states: "to us of the 1950s any recognition, let alone admission, of homosexual urges would have scared the living shit out of us. I think we were very much into a one-shot deviance model when I was growing up. One use of drugs, particularly marijuana, made you a confirmed junkie. The same with homosexual activities; one contact and the stigma popped right up on your face, like an outbreak of 'zits'."

Socioeconomic class partly explains our discreet silence. And date of birth largely explains that the silence is concealing not the secret but the absence of homosexuality. We were born too early for the gay revolution. Having said all this, however, I would also say that we have been reticent about sexuality not only because we are middle class and of a certain age, but because we are men. Recently I participated with four other men in a day-long workshop to discuss sexual questions and fears. After eight hours we acknowledged that we had shared many fears and questions, theories and insights, but somehow had managed to avoid mentioning anything graphically physical or taboo. Women, so I'm told, have much less difficulty in talking about their bodies—perhaps because they feel less pressure to perform and succeed in bed.

MISSING PARTS   But one can exaggerate the meanings of silence. And this is, after all, a book not about sexuality but about work and family. If something significant is missing, it concerns an area more intangible than genitals. As Harry Boyte observed, "There is a feeling of loss that comes through in the essays, of some sadness and hints of loneliness. A central theme for them all is the struggle for *recovery*, struggling to recover more personal, emotional, playful parts of ourselves that our academic/professional/male training actively suppressed. There is also a reappropriation of our pasts, a form of self-acceptance about our needs for achievement, our families and their values, our history—even when we seek to go beyond them."

He has touched, I think, upon an elusive and complex current running beneath the surface of the prose. On the one hand, most of us profess to be or would wish to be dissidents, breaking the conventional mold and freeing the insurgent emotions and possibilities within us. On the other hand, our stories contain a remarkable stability: in our marriages, we have accommodated and respected women who are assertively autonomous; in our careers we have found ways to mesh personal needs with outward achievement. As Lawrence Rubin remarks, "Every one of us want to adhere ultimately to traditional responsibility, dependability, and respectability. In that sense, we end up imitating our parents. Maybe better than them, maybe not, but—so far one can discern through the differences of language that have grown up between the generations—we seem to become much like our parents."

Is some profound confusion of purposes at work, confounding our efforts at self-realization? Perhaps. But a more generous and optimistic interpretation is that we are trying to *contain* this interior diversity—to own the fullness of who we are and have been. A recovery of suppressed emotions. A reappropriation of our diverse parts. A reintegration of our past and present relationships as sons, husbands, and fathers.

Although using different words and emphases, all of the contributors agree that we are engaged in this process of reintegration. But we disagree on which factors are propelling or impeding the process. Some analyze it in terms of gender—as a process of male liberation. Others see it in terms of age—as a process of midlife transition.

MEN'S LIBERATION?   "Hmm, men's liberation," Arn Strasser muses. "I'm glad none of the essays used the label, since that created a refreshing lack of rhetoric. But I suppose 'men's liberation' is as good as any label to describe breaking the shackles of sexism, machismo, and competition. Now, you ask me, do I feel 'liberated'? My first response is, 'I'm struggling to be liberated.' But that implies guilt and seems again like pat rhetoric. All in all, yes, I would say I'm a liberated man. There—I've said it, and it feels *good.*"

Steve Turner sees the question in more complicated and chastening ways. "I don't think liberation is the appropriate word. *Relief* seems more appropriate, or perhaps *relaxation.* Liberation conveys lightness, joy, and victoriousness that doesn't necessarily result from the process of shedding the bindings of male privilege and dominance. Men whose living patterns are strongly adjusted to assumptions of male privilege, for instance, inevitably experience some combination of confusion, anger, and grief during reorientation. Additionally, as Hahn indicates so clearly, the transition away from sexist practice is likely to heat up shame from the realization of what a shit you've been—or at least what patterns of shit you have accepted and enjoyed.

"Moreover, liberation carries the suggestion of a solution to the problem: relationships between 'liberated' men and women by implication, should be less stressful than unliberated relationships, and that just isn't the case. If anything, the conflicts of new adjustment may easily outweigh (just as they surely outdistance) the original reasons for having a relationship at all.

"In the fullest sense, I think, struggling to become a nonsexist man is an attempt to become not just a freer and gentler spirit, but a more responsible *social* individual. The outcome hopefully includes the former goal, and yields a fuller life in the bargain. But it doesn't yield an easier life, because the expanded focus means more complex, more engrossing relationships with other people, and more perceptive involvement in coping with the social forces shaping those relationships. Equal status relationships involve the greatest investment of time, energy, and emotional commitment. Nurturance, that most romanticized of feminine prerogatives in sexist society, brings (as any mother can tell you) as much trouble as joy. And releasing the emotions, learning to cry and admit despair, opens up a new set of contacts with other people (unless you do your crying alone) that can burn or drain on occasion, as well as comfort."

OR MIDLIFE TRANSITION? Tom Kreilkamp "would definitely describe myself as a liberated man," at least in the conventional meaning of breaking out of stereotyped roles at home and work. But gender interests him less than age. "Growing older is an important issue for me, because it has brought me a growing strength. When I was younger, I used to have infinite expectations. Only gradually have I been able to gain a sense of what a day or a week or a year might offer. When I was twenty or so, I feared that everything was stuck in some endless stasis. Gradually I have begun to realize that life does not go on forever, nor will it end tomorrow. My children contribute to this sense of movement because their growth is so vivid, so manifestly obvious. All in all, I gather strength from the passage of time now, because I have gained a clearer sense of what it means to have my own life."

Strangely enough, Paul Fiddleman declares the same clarity but takes it as a cue for brooding dejection. I say it is "strange" because he and Kreilkamp had identified so strongly with each other's essays, recognizing a shared tone and attitude. But as Kreilkamp smoothly joins the motion of middle-aged time, Fiddleman stumbles upon worries. "I wonder sometimes if my coming to grips with myself, and feeling that I have finally accepted what and who I am, warts and all, hasn't been without its cost. When stress has been overcome, do we lose some energy or motivation? If we no longer have to hunt fresh meat and only have to wait for the delivery van, will we lose the need for meat and then begin to find counterfeit challenges and straw men to attack and destroy? Or, to carry my earlier analogy up to the present, if we hit enough crossroads and make enough decisions, do we eventually become so practiced that we always make the appropriate choices? I would hate to live vicariously through others' failures and successes, only having my own dated war stories to tell an increasingly bored audience. I guess what I am realizing is that my title may not be so accurate after all. After finally humping it over the hump, I may find that the worst thing that can happen is to have no hump at all."

Perhaps the surprising divergence between these two psychologists can be explained by the fact that Fiddleman is seven years older (born in 1934) and therefore farther into middle age. In other words, men's attitudes are shaped by their gender but increasingly re-shaped by time. This is a hypothesis that deserves to be tested. But one thing is certain: we are doubly "men in the middle." We are undergoing a drastic realignment of male and female roles, and at the same time, as we grow toward forty and beyond, we are undergoing a disquieting revision of self-in-time.

We confront the sex-role issue with general agreement on the terms to be used and the goals to be sought. We confront the issue of aging, however, with considerable disagreement or we don't confront it at all. Why the contrast? For one thing, we are all men but we are not all the same age—seven or eight years seem to make a large difference. Moreover, we have all wrestled with sexism for almost a decade, beginning with the challenge from "liberated" women and continuing among ourselves. But we have wrestled with middle age for only a brief time, if at all, so the questions are less clear, the objectives more uncertain.

Robert Hahn captures this protean quality when he asks "What does it feel like to feel one's age? Norman Mailer points out that we carry about selves of various ages within us at all times. There is a part of me which is a terrified twelve. Part is a buoyant twenty, all promise and potential, everything ahead. A troublesome part thinks of itself as forty-going-on-fifty-five, as if this gradient were a sharp declivity down which former plans and pleasures rush away. There is something to be learned from this forty-going-on-fifty-five time-self, but mainly it strikes me as a pernicious enemy. This flabby tempter invites me to give up the struggle to live day by day."

FAREWELL, FELLOW READER, HELLO   We are not sure where we are going, but we presume that we are in the middle of the journey. Our lives have not ended.

This book has ended, but we hope it has sequels in the lives of our readers. "It seems to me," Steve Turner concludes, "that we offer a tolerable case study for people interested in such things. And if it's others like us who mostly end up reading this book, here's a hello from me." And from us.